1992 Talya Looem

Critical Guides to German Texts

11 Mann: Mario und der Zauberer

Critical Guides to German Texts

EDITED BY MARTIN SWALES

MANN

Mario und der Zauberer

Ronald Speirs

Reader in German
University of Birmingham

Grant & Cutler Ltd
1990

I.S.B.N. 84-599-3068-8

DEPÓSITO LEGAL: V. 1.701 - 1990

Printed in Spain by
Artes Gráficas Soler, S.A., Valencia
for
GRANT & CUTLER LTD
55-57, GREAT MARLBOROUGH STREET, LONDON W1V 2AY

Contents

Note on References   7

Preface   8

Introduction   9

1. The Rise of Fascism in Italy and National
       Socialism in Germany   11

2. The Political Context in *Mario und der Zauberer*   14

3. The Social Psychology of Fascism   22

4. The Magician   27

5. The Leader and the Led   31

6. Myth   37

7. Culture and Politics   43

8. The Problem of Freedom   48

9. The Role of the Narrator   56

10. The Role of Mario   60

11. Aspects of Narration
       The Illusion of Reality   67
       Genre   72
       Artistic Integration   75
       Leitmotif and Symbol   77
       Complexity and Irony   82

Bibliography   88

Note on References

The page numbers in brackets in this text refer to pages of *Mario und der Zauberer* in the 1987 paperback edition of *Unordnung und frühes Leid und andere Erzählungen* (Fischer Taschenbuch Verlag). Other references, indicated in brackets by italicized figures, are to the numbered items in the Bibliography.

Preface

It may be of some comfort to the English-speaking students of German to know that Thomas Mann's German readers too find that he is a demanding writer. Demanding but rewarding. The difficulties, whether of language or of content, are a matter of complexity rather than obscurity. The present study aims to help the reader appreciate one of Mann's subtlest and most complex stories (second perhaps only to *Der Tod in Venedig* as a masterpiece of his short fiction) by separating out various themes and levels of meaning in the story — political, philosophical, psychological. This dissecting approach leaves me feeling uneasy, however, since the distinction of Mann's art lies precisely in the ability to convey many meanings simultaneously, as elements in a complex, evolving whole. Having analysed a good number of the parts, I must leave it to the reader to gain his or her own sense of the whole.

The preparatory work for this study took me back to Zürich, where I was once a student. I should like to thank the University of Birmingham for the research grant that enabled me to visit the Thomas Mann Archiv of the Eidgenössische Technische Hochschule, and to express my gratitude to Professor Wysling and Frau Hiltermann for their kindness and practical help during that visit.

Introduction

Thomas Mann began to write *Mario und der Zauberer* in circumstances that mirrored those in which he had originally experienced the events underlying the story. In August 1929 Mann was holidaying at Bad Rauschen on the Baltic coast, having reluctantly forsaken the pleasures of the warmer Italian resorts as a result of the family's unpleasant experiences during their holiday at Forte dei Marmi in 1926. That holiday had been marred from the outset by a new hostility towards foreigners which was part of the increasingly nationalistic mood of the Italians:

> An kleinen Widerwärtigkeiten hat es anfangs auch nicht gefehlt, die mit dem derzeitigen unerfreulichen überspannten und fremdenfeindlichen nationalen Gemütszustand zusammenhingen, und uns belehrten, daß man jetzt nicht gut tut, einen Badeort dieses Landes in der rein italienischen Hochsaison aufzusuchen. (*87*, pp.24f.)

During that holiday the family attended a performance by a hypnotist-magician which Mann, taking up a suggestion provided by his daughter Erika, used as the central symbolic event in his imaginative reworking of the experience. This task of reflection and reconstruction was greatly facilitated by the familiar sights and sounds of the sea, for they linked the past holiday with the present so powerfully that the story almost seemed to write itself:

> Ich rückte den Sitzkorb nah an den Saum des Wassers...und so...ließ ich es geschehen, daß mir aus der Anekdote die Fabel, aus lockerer Mitteilsamkeit die geistige Erzählung, aus dem Privaten das Ethisch-Symbolische unversehens erwuchs, — während immerfort

ein glückliches Erstaunen darüber mich erfüllte, wie doch
das Meer jede menschliche Störung zu absorbieren und in
seine geliebte Ungeheuerlichkeit aufzulösen vermag.
(*7*, p.367)

Such symbolic repetitions of experience were already an
established part of Mann's artistic and personal existence, but in
this case the outward correspondence between the northern
resort where the story was conceived and the southern resort
where the original events took place was given an added, far
from pleasant significance by the fact that social and
psychological conditions in the Germany of 1929 had become
worryingly similar to those Mann had experienced in Italy three
years previously. To be more precise, what the story had to
report about life in Italy, where a fascist regime was firmly
entrenched by 1929, was addressed to the reading public in
Thomas Mann's native Germany where fascist tendencies, in the
shape of National Socialism, had not *yet* become the dominant
force in the life of society, but where Mann had reason to fear
they might become so.

Yet although *Mario und der Zauberer* undoubtedly is a story
with strong political overtones ('eine stark ins Politische
hinüberspielende Geschichte, *3*, p.679), it is, as Mann warned
his interpreters, far from being a simple 'tagespolitische
Allegorie' (*7*, p.371) or a fable with an easily applicable moral.
Indeed the story's *refusal* to deal in simplifications is an
important aspect of the contribution it makes to the processes of
'Selbstkritik und Selbstkorrektur' (*11*, p.80) which Mann
considered essential to the health of society, particularly at a
time when many 'terribles simplificateurs' were peddling
seductively easy solutions to profound social and cultural
problems. Because the story stands in an oblique, complicated
relationship to the sphere of politics it will be necessary to
consider not only the factual background of political
developments in Italy and Germany against which the events of
the story are set, but also the wide range of literary,
philosophical, psychological, cultural and social reflections
Mann subsequently brought to bear on the experiences of that
unhappy holiday in Forte dei Marmi.

1. The Rise of Fascism in Italy and National Socialism in Germany

Benito Mussolini, leader of the Italian fascist movement, was handed the seals of office to govern Italy by the country's weak and vacillating King Victor Emanuel III on 29 October 1922. The immediate occasion of the king's surrender of power to Mussolini was the so-called 'March on Rome' on October 28th, when between ten and twenty thousand fascists, armed with revolvers or sticks, assembled in the suburbs of Rome, the majority having not marched but travelled there by road and rail. Had the king been less easily intimidated by the fascists' record of violence, and had he granted to the ruling prime minister, Facta, a decree declaring martial law, the fascist threat might well have been eliminated there and then by the rapid deployment of military force (see King, *26*, p.27). As it was, Mussolini, once given a formal hold on power, proceeded to make his power total, stifling opposition through the brutality of his Black Shirts, the suppression of freedom of speech and the progressive destruction of the institutions of democratic government. By 1929, when Mann came to write about his experiences, Mussolini was able to declare that in Italy the state and fascism were identical.

The roots of Italian fascism reached back into the early years of the First World War. The country had initially been reluctant to join the Entente forces in the war against Germany, but was forced into participation by a mood of discontent fomented by fervent nationalists, notably Mussolini and the poet Gabriele D'Annunzio, with their invocations of the lost glories of the Roman imperial past. In the early period of hostilities, however, these claims that Italy was heir to a tradition of military greatness contrasted embarrassingly with the all too evident lack of success enjoyed by a spiritless and disunited Italian army that eventually broke up ignominiously under pressure at Caporetto. After that it rallied to some extent, although never to the extent of covering itself in military glory as the fascists, bent on puffing up patriotic pride, were later to claim. To add insult to injury, the spoils of war also failed to match the expectations raised by the expansionist nationalists, for the Entente powers denied Italy the right to annexe Dalmatia or even the city of Fiume. To national resentment at the 'lost peace' was added the fear, felt particularly by the middle and upper classes, that radical socialists, in imitation of the Bolshevik revolution of 1917 in Russia, might seize control of the country in the chaotic aftermath of the war. When, in 1919, Italian peasants and workers began to seize land, to strike and to occupy factories, groups of fascists, equipped from army stores and well financed by the 'possessing classes' (King, *26*, p.24), countered with a campaign of terror against socialists and their sympathizers, ostensibly to 'save the nation' but in fact with the aim of seizing power themselves and imposing on their countrymen the rule of fear founded on an ideology of hatred that is the hallmark of fascism.

In contrast to the surprising ease with which the 'March on Rome' brought success to Mussolini and his followers, the first attempt by Adolf Hitler and his National Socialists (NSDAP) to emulated the Italian example with their so-called 'Munich putsch' in November 1923 ended in abject failure with the banning of the NSDAP and the arrest and imprisonment of Hitler in Landsberg fortress until December 1924. However, those who thought that the Munich débâcle, the waning of popular support in the mid-twenties for the 'Völkischen', and internal divisions in the movement meant that the threat from National Socialism had simply dissolved into farce were to be proved wrong by subsequent events.[1] Like the fascists in Italy, the National Socialists had gained considerable support in the immediate aftermath of the war by appealing to feelings of

[1] Fabry (*21*, *passim*) documents the widespread underestimation of Hitler and Nazism throughout the 1920s. Mann deserves great credit for taking the threat of fascism so seriously at a time when both Hitler and Mussolini were often seen as comic figures; hence the lack of 'Clownerie' in Cipolla's attitude (*17*, p.234).

anger at the country's defeat — or, as they would have it, the fact that the German army had been 'stabbed in the back' by the politicians at home — and to widespread German resentment of the economic chaos that had been created after the war by the burden of reparations payments and runaway inflation. The Nazis, with their ever-ready tactic of focussing national discontent on some convenient scapegoat, blamed these problems entirely on the Jews and on an alleged conspiracy of 'international capitalism'. Yet, though the relative stabilization of German economic and political life in the mid-twenties caused the resentments exploited by the Nazis to abate for a while (and Nazi electoral support to drop sharply in 1928), Hitler and his cohorts were able to rekindle those emotions rapidly at the end of the decade when the Young Plan (1929) brought the question of German reparations back into political focus, and Germany's economic development again took a sharp turn for the worse, with unemployment once more soaring to disastrously high levels, particularly after the Wall Street Crash of 1929 (see *20*, pp.267-326). Like the Italian fascists, the Nazis used as their main political weapons outright physical violence against their opponents (particularly against the Communists, their main rivals for the popular vote), and the unscrupulous rhetoric of Adolf Hitler and Joseph Goebbels (*Gauleiter* of Berlin from 1926 and subsequent 'Reichsminister für Volksaufklärung und Propaganda'). What these men wrote and said was calculated to whip up national self-pity and to channel the accompanying compensatory feelings of anger into hatred of the Nazis' chosen scapegoats: Jews, Bolsheviks and, of course, the Entente powers for having supposedly desecrated the honour of the German people with their 'shameful' Treaty of Versailles.

2. *The Political Context in* Mario und der Zauberer

In *Mario und der Zauberer* this background of political events is largely taken for granted, presumably because the author believed that contemporary readers would be bound to be familiar with such things.[2] On the other hand, although the story's political points are mainly conveyed by means of symbolic allusion, Mann supplied a number of quite clear and direct pointers to the political context of the events narrated, so as to create for the reader a firm frame of reference within which to interpret those allusions and suggestions.

From an early stage in his evening of entertainment, explicit references to the wider background of patriotic politics are an important element in the 'illusionist' Cipolla's banter with his audience. The magician expresses regret, for example, that physical disability prevented him 'am Kriege für die Größe des Vaterlandes teilzunehmen' (p.238), but goes on to point out, by way of compensation, that his artistic work has earned him recognition not only from the country's educated classes ('der gebildeten Öffentlichkeit') but also from the 'Bruder des Duce' in Rome. Cipolla again invokes the greatness of the fatherland, and of Rome in particular, when, on learning that two young citizens of Torre di Venere are unable to write on the blackboard, he protests that this is scandalous in a country like Italy, 'dessen Größe der Unwissenheit und Finsternis keinen Raum bietet', and denounces their illiteracy as a failing 'mit der ihr nicht nur euch selbst erniedrigt, sondern auch die Regierung und das Land dem Gerede aussetzt' (p.243). By contrast, Cipolla is delighted to be able to reveal to his audience Signora Angiolieri's connection with the distinguished actress Eleonora Duse, whose 'Ruhm sich längst mit dem des Vaterlandes verbunden hat und mit ihm unsterblich ist' (p.255). As Cipolla has surely intended, the public's response to this announce-

[2] Mann's regular readers, at any rate, would have been aware from his speeches and essays of the political orientation of his thinking; contrast Freese (*64, passim*).

ment 'glich einer nationalen Kundgebung' (p.255).[3] The contemporary significance of all these references to national glory is signalled most clearly at the climax of the evening's entertainment, when Cipolla, on making the acquaintance of the waiter Mario, greets him repeatedly with the fascist salute and praises him for bearing a name so redolent of the nation's heroic traditions:

> 'Ein verbreiteter Name. Ein antiker Name, einer von denen, die die heroischen Überlieferungen des Vaterlandes wach erhalten. Bravo. Salve!' Und er streckte Arm und flache Hand aus seiner schiefen Schulter zum römischen Gruß schräg aufwärts. (p.269)

Although Cipolla in a sense brings the new fascist regime in Rome onto his little stage by copying the 'römischen Gruß', it is important to recognize that the nationalist mood in the public is not actually created by him. Rather he simply exploits for his own ends the social and psychological conditions which Mussolini's regime has already brought about, the effects of which have become apparent in Torre di Venere long before the magician makes his appearance there.[4] In fact, from the very beginning of their stay in the town the narrator and his family have been made uncomfortably aware of an unfamiliar air of pronounced nationalism amongst the Italians: 'Man verstand bald, daß Politisches umging, die Idee der Nation im Spiele war' (p.224). As a result of this new mood they are treated as second-rate guests in the Grand Hôtel, firstly by being refused permission to dine on the veranda because, they are informed, this is a privilege reserved 'ai nostri clienti' (p.218) — 'for our own (i.e. Italian) guests' — and then by being required to move into an annexe simply to please an Italian aristocrat who objects to their presence in the room next to her own. The prevailing

---

[3] As Müller-Salget has pointed out (*86*, p.55), Duse's affair with the pro-fascist D'Annunzio was also public knowledge. Forte dei Marmi, incidentally, was one of D'Annunzio's haunts.

[4] Contrast Sautermeister (*89*, p.56), who claims that the early part of the story shows both 'die Vorgeschichte des Faschismus' and 'Nebenwirkungen des Faschismus'.

antipathy towards foreigners even affects the Italian children, making them so patriotic that they quarrel too readily with children from other countries:

> Es gab Empfindlichkeiten...einen Flaggenzwist, Streit-
> fragen des Ansehens und Vorranges; Erwachsene mischten
> sich weniger schlichtend als entscheidend und Grundsätze
> wahrend ein, Redensarten von der Größe und Würde
> Italiens fielen, unheiter-spielverderberische Redensarten
> (pp.224f.)[5]

The German visitors are then treated to an example of the kind of adult behaviour on which the Italian children have presumably modelled theirs. When the narrator's little daughter unwittingly offends against current standards of propriety in Italy the family is berated by an indignant Italian for their 'Mißbrauch der Gastfreundschaft Italiens', and for slighting 'die Ehre seines Landes' (p.226). Nor is this outburst some individual foible, for not only is their accuser supported by the other Italians in the vicinity, but his views are also endorsed by local officials who lecture the German visitors 'in genau denselben, offenbar landläufigen didaktischen Redewendungen' (p.227), and then impose a fine on them for committing this supposedly 'molto grave' offence. Clearly then the values, attitudes and language of ordinary Italians have been pervasively influenced by Mussolini's fascist ideology long before Cipolla arrives in Torre di Venere to practise *his* brand of malicious sorcery.

Although Cipolla cannot be identified in any straight-forwardly allegorical way with Mussolini, he is nevertheless linked to the *Duce*, and other fascist leaders, by a series of detailed symbolic allusions. Mann's choice of an evening at the theatre as the setting for his story, for example, provides an important link between the magician and the dictator in that it clearly calls to mind the notorious theatricality of Mussolini's political style — his seemingly inexhaustible wardrobe of

[5] The effects of fascism on the behaviour of children also struck other foreign visitors; see Mack Smith (*29*, p.161).

flamboyant uniforms, his 'poses of the inherent actor, with chest thrown out and bulbous chin pointed to the sky' (Massock, *30*, p.5), the calculated use of symbolism to drive home the message of fascism with clarity and emotive force, the carefully stage-managed public rallies, the high, elaborate rostrum incorporating a huge, threatening fascist emblem of an axe bound up in a bundle of rods (a design borrowed from ancient Rome).[6] The effect of such theatricality on an already theatrically disposed people is indicated in the story — again before Cipolla's arrival — when a minor accident suffered by the repulsive and attention-seeking bully Fuggiero produces an equally histrionic response from the adults who then carry him shoulder-high from the beach as if he were some hero fallen in battle.

As with his allusions to the theatricality of fascist politics, Mann was drawing on an already well-established way of talking about Mussolini (the 'entrancer' of the Italian people) when he based his satirical study of the arts of demagogy on his observations of a hypnotist. There are various such allusions which are easy to identify, while others seem to be based on the relatively obscure kind of symbolic detail Thomas Mann was in the habit of giving his readers to puzzle over. Cipolla's invocations of the power of the will (particularly his own), for example, can be related fairly easily to Mussolini's frequent public references to this concept, but it demands a rather more detailed knowledge of Mussolini's career to recognize in Cipolla's stage-props (a table and blackboard which make the stage resemble 'eher einer Schulstube als dem Wirkungsfeld eines Taschenspielers', p.232) a possible reference to the dictator's early years as schoolmaster, when (as Mack Smith has suggested — *29*, p.130) he probably developed the hectoring manner — at times even with raised, wagging finger — which he still used in his political speeches. The suggested parallel is then strengthened by the way Cipolla scolds two lumbering Italian 'Trottel' for their illiteracy, sending them back to their seats

---

[6] Walter Benjamin characterized such techniques as 'Ästhetisierung der Politik' (*35*, p.175). This concept is central to Sautermeister's interpretation of the role of Cipolla (*89*, p.64).

('Geht an eure Plätze!', p.243) like a pair of stupid schoolboys.

Thomas Mann once wrote that the story did not take shape in his mind until his eldest daughter, on hearing about the real events at the hypnotist's show in Forte dei Marmi, exclaimed that she would not have been surprised if the magician had been shot for his humiliation of the waiter (see 7, p.368). One wonders whether Mann might not also have been influenced to use her suggestion by the fact that there were several much publicized attempts to assassinate Mussolini in 1926, one of which actually occurred during the holiday (September 11th), while another, carried out by a young man who was immediately lynched by a fascist mob, took place just over a month later, on October 31st (see 19, p.253).

Like Mussolini, who 'liked to think of himself as a man excluded from communion with others' (29, p.110), Cipolla is an isolated figure. On the other hand, just as Mussolini saw himself as speaking for the Italian people, especially its youth (the fascist rallying song was entitled 'Giovinezza'), Cipolla repeatedly addresses himself to the young men in the audience, his first victim being a lad by the name of *Giovan*otto who shows himself to be a fascist enthusiast by sporting 'die Modefrisur des erweckten Vaterlandes' (p.236)[7] — a connection repeatedly stressed by references such as 'Giovanotto mit der kriegerischen Haartracht' (p.267) or 'Giovanotto mit der Kriegs-frisur' (p.270). Cipolla's 'metallic'-sounding voice resembles Mussolini's (see 19, p.269), while his severe look ('strenge Ernsthaftigkeit, Ablehnung alles Humoristischen', p.234) is similarly modelled on the *Duce* who reportedly censored photographs which showed him smiling (see 29, p.110). Even the rather incongruous riding crop with which Cipolla controls his audience may allude to Mussolini's liking for appearing before the public in jodphurs or on horseback (thus disguising his shortness of physical stature), while the claw-shaped handle of the whip hints at the rapacious imperial eagle depicted in many fascist (and Nazi) emblems. Mussolini's first biography ends with his reported 'desire to impose himself on the century like a

7 The phrase 'des erweckten Vaterlandes' recalls the Nazi slogan 'Deutschland, erwache!'

lion with its claw (see *29*, p.114); according to Fermi he also had 'the Roman eagle placed in a cage on the Capitol' (*22*, p.219) and kept a lioness named 'Italia' (*22*, p.275).

Although the parallels between Cipolla and Mussolini are numerous and detailed, it would be wrong, as Mann once observed, 'in dem Zauberer Cipolla einfach eine Maskierung Mussolinis zu sehen' (*87*, p.48), for there are also important differences between the two figures, some of which have to do with the fact that Mann's concerns in this story were not exclusively political, while others have to do with the fact that he did not consider fascism to be an exclusively Italian phenomenon. Cipolla's physical build, for example, is quite unlike Mussolini's. Whereas Mussolini, although rather short, was a powerfully built man who even strove to give an impression of athleticism (see *29*, p.106), Cipolla's body is expressly that of a 'Krüppel' (p.248). The physical defect which, as he complains, prevented him from fighting in the war, is an unusual deformity of the *lower* spine ('eine Art Hüft- und Gesäßbuckel', p.240) which affects very noticeably the way he walks: 'grotesk und bei jedem Schritt sonderbar ausladend' (p.240). When taken together with certain other details, this striking and abnormal gait suggests that the figure may also have been modelled on Joseph Goebbels, already a prominent figure in the Nazi party by the time the story came to be written. Goebbels, who had a disproportionately large head and a club foot, had to learn (like Cipolla) how to deal with the laughter which often greeted him when he hobbled awkwardly onto a platform to speak. As Heiber reports, it was in part this deformity, and in part his mixture of arrogance, malevolence and cunning, that earned Goebbels the nickname of 'Mephistopheles' among allies and enemies alike (see *23*, p.12). His deformity is often offered too as an explanation for his pursuit of power by the use of his intellectual and oratorical abilities. Cipolla's praise of his own achievements ('Allein mit den Kräften meiner Seele und meines Geistes meistere ich das Leben', p.238) could equally well have come from the lips of Goebbels.

It is perhaps surprising that Cipolla bears so little outward resemblance to Adolf Hitler, particularly as Thomas Mann's place of residence until 1933 was Munich, the Bavarian capital where the Nazi movement had its seat. As a well informed and critical resident of that city, Mann was well aware of Hitler and the activities of his 'Brownshirts' there. It seems to me very likely that Mann had a strong aversion to depicting in his artistic work a man whom he loathed with the utmost intensity, for when he returned, in his novel *Doktor Faustus* (1947), to the analogy between political and satanic corruption within a specifically German context, he again created a 'Mephistopheles' with no obvious physical similarity to Hitler. On the other hand certain features of Cipolla's performance, such as the insalubrious locale, the lateness of the appointed hour and the deliberately delayed appearance of the speaker, were all part of Hitler's demagogic stock-in-trade, while rumours about his alleged sexual abnormality (variously interpreted as impotence or homosexuality) circulated from an early date in his public career. More important than these details, however, is the extent to which Mann's later study of Hitler's character, in a famous essay entitled 'Ein Bruder' (subsequently retitled 'Bruder Hitler'), is already anticipated by his analysis of Cipolla's motivation in *Mario*. Mann saw in Hitler, as in Cipolla, a distorted, pathological expression of the artistic mentality, one which seeks to remould the world in accordance with the dictates of a wounded subjectivity and to compensate for low self-esteem by the pursuit of power:

> ...muß man nicht, ob man will oder nicht, in dem Phänomen eine Erscheinungsform des Künstlertums wiedererkennen?...die unterbewußte Ansammlung explosiver Kompensationswünsche, das zäh arbeitende Bedürfnis, sich zu rechtfertigen, zu beweisen, der Drang zur Überwältigung, Unterwerfung, der Traum, eine in Angst, Liebe, Bewunderung, Scham vergehende Welt zu den Füßen des einst Verschmähten zu sehen. (*10*, Vol.2, p.224)

What emerges then from the various similarities and differences between Cipolla and the most prominent representatives of Italian and German fascism? Firstly, it is clear that Cipolla is a composite figure rather than a portrait of one particular politician. Secondly, it is important to recognize that Cipolla is not at the centre of political power but operates as a subordinate figure within a society where the rule of fascism is already established. This conception of the figure enabled Mann to offer a suggestive study of dictatorship in miniature, while at the same time absolving him of any obligation to give a precise and comprehensive account of the establishment and operation of actual political dictatorship. It also permitted him to build into the figure allusions to other spheres of life — cultural, philosophical, ethical and mythological — which have political implications without being directly political. For all its 'kleine politische Glanzlichter und Anspielungen aktueller Art' (7, p.370), *Mario und der Zauberer* relates to the sphere of politics by partial analogy rather than as a strict allegory.

3. The Social Psychology of Fascism

Mario und der Zauberer does more than simply allude to the fascist background of the events in Torre di Venere. The story attempts to illuminate fascism from a psychological and moral point of view by exploring the interrelatedness of dominant and submissive behaviour in this particular type of society. To understand the power of Cipolla over his audience one needs to begin by analysing the conditions prevailing in Torre di Venere before the magician's arrival in town, since these conditions lay the foundations of his success.

The opening sentences of the story dwell on the unpleasant atmosphere of 'Ärger, Gereiztheit, Überspannung' (p.215) that dominates the narrator's memory of the holiday, a widespread mood of irritability which later seemed to be concentrated and embodied in the person of Cipolla. As he recalls various details and incidents of the holiday, the narrator attributes the prevailing mood of irritation to a variety of causes. The first is the overcrowding of the resort. Like all such resorts, Torre is mainly frequented by city-dwellers looking for peace and an escape from the hectic, unnatural and overcrowded environment in which they normally live. Ironically but inevitably, however, these crowds of visitors dispel, by their own presence, the very peace they have come in search of. If anything, these city-dwellers transform small holiday resorts into crucibles where the tensions of modern, urban existence are increased rather than relaxed, as masses of people are crowded together in the cafés and on the streets and beaches so that there is no avoiding the jostling of those 'others' one has come here to get away from. The narrator's vivid recollection of the annoyances of life on the beach — the infernal heat and din, the harsh colours, the coarse behaviour and hectic activity of beach touts and holidaymakers alike ('es wimmelte von zeterndem, zankendem, jauchzendem

Badevolk', p.216) — makes it clear why everyone there is so irritable and quarrelsome. Even in the surrounding countryside the restless city-dwellers who seek solace in unspoiled nature find only frustration, as the dusty vegetation only reminds the 'Freunde des unverweltlichten Elements' (p.216) of the ubiquitous, suffocating effects of modern civilization:

> ...dank den hin und her sausenden Fiat-Wagen ist das Lorbeer- und Oleandergebüsch am Saum der verbindenden Landstraße von weißem Staube zolldick verschneit — ein merkwürdiger, aber abstoßender Anblick. (p.217)

Thus the story is by no means confined in its implications to Italy, for the events in Torre di Venere are partly the consequence of potentially dangerous frustrations inherent in any modern society.

Nevertheless, for a potential danger to become an actual danger, something must happen to precipitate it. In Italy at the time of the narrator's visit the necessary conditions have been created by the influence of Mussolini's regime on the Italian people. As we have seen, the narrator and his family encounter at every turn a mood of hostile, self-assertive nationalism amongst Italians. Fascism, in other words, has channelled into officially endorsed jingoism the latent aggression produced on the one hand by the general frustrations of modern life and on the other by the humiliating aspects of Italy's recent history. To compensate for their sense of inferiority in the eyes of other nations, the Italians are only too eager to listen to Mussolini's invocations of the glories of the nation's past, and to seize any opportunity to reassert their injured national pride, particularly in the presence of foreigners. All this forms the implicit background to experiences which oblige the narrator and his family to leave the Grand Hôtel after their double humiliation there, first in the incident concerning the veranda and then, more seriously, when they are asked to move out to an annexe.

This latter incident reveals two further important characteristics of life under fascism. The first is the flourishing of an attitude of corrupt subservience ('der kriecherischen

Korruption', p.221) towards the social elite. The second is the strong element of irrationality in the behaviour of the Italians. The princess's ostensible motive for wanting the German family moved to other rooms is her fear that her own children will be infected aurally by the nocturnal coughing of one of the narrator's children who has recently suffered a bout of whooping cough. This is superstitious nonsense, of course, but although the woman's fears are dismissed as groundless by a doctor, the manager remains adamant (presumably on her insistence) that the German family must move to other rooms. Ironically, her groundless fear of physical contagion from others suggests that she herself is already infected by the moral disease of irrational xenophobia that is rampant amongst her countrymen.

The evident discrepancy between the explicit and the actual motives of the princess is a behavioural trait encountered repeatedly by the narrator in Torre di Venere, the most striking example being the angry response of some Italians on the beach to the sight of the narrator's little daughter running naked down to the sea. Not only is this a case of nationalist hostility finding ostensibly legitimate expression in a show of moral outrage, it also reveals one of the unacknowledged psychological mainsprings of that aggression. Although initially taken aback by this apparent 'Rückschlag von Prüderie und Über-empfindlichkeit' (p.227), the narrator is quick to identify the cause of the overreaction, recognizing the little Italian's outburst to be, 'eine Philippika...in der alles Pathos des sinnenfreudigen Südens sich in den Dienst spröder Zucht und Sitte gestellt findet' (p.226). The perceptiveness of this comment, incidentally, is confirmed by the historian Mack Smith who records that fascist 'puritanical strictness revealed itself in an attempt to regulate women's fashions and behaviour. Prudish rules were prescribed for the shape of bathing costumes and the length of skirts' (*29*, p.161).

The behaviour observed by the narrator is symptomatic of what Freudian psychologists define as the processes of repression, displacement and sublimation. According to Freudian theory, to which Mann was very sympathetic, when a strong desire or impulse (in this case, 'Sinnenfreude') is denied its direct, natural form of expression, the emotional energy of the original impulse does not simply disappear but rather is redirected into the service of some other, supposedly higher value (in this case, the honour of the Italian nation). Yet, like Freud, Thomas Mann was keenly aware that deep emotional impulses, particularly those connected with sexuality (this is implied in the symbolic name 'Torre di *Venere*'), are very resistant to any such enforced sublimation. His stories repeatedly show that denying human needs their natural outlet is likely to result in frustration which in turn seeks an outlet in some form of aggression towards others: the pain of self-denial demands compensation in suffering inflicted on someone else. Hence the 'Pathos' or passionate intensity of the Italian's 'moral' outburst in which he discharges as anger the normally harmless feelings of pleasure in the human body that have been severely constrained by the fascist ideology of discipline and austerity.[8] The unnaturalness produced by the new ethos is also reflected in the behaviour of the aggressively 'patriot-ischen Kindern — eine unnatürliche und niederschlagende Erscheinung' (p.224) and by the incongruous frock-coat and bowler-hat worn — on the beach of all places — by the irate Italian.[9]

The repressed, unnatural condition of the Italians is further manifested in the way they lay claim to a 'self' that is more a matter of show than of substance:

Auf irgendeine Weise fehlte es der Atmosphäre an Unschuld, an Zwanglosigkeit; dies Publikum 'hielt auf sich' — man wußte zunächst nicht recht, in welchem Sinn und Geist, es prästierte Würde, stellte voreinander und vor dem Fremden Ernst und Haltung, wach aufgerichtete Ehrliebe zur Schau (p.224)

[8] Fascist prudery was accompanied by a cult of the body, but as an instrument of athletic or military prowess rather than as a source of sensuous pleasure. Mann shared Nietzsche's profound suspicion of all forms of asceticism: 'Radikale Askese, das bedeutet immer und überall nur Charakterschwäche' (*13*, p.55).

[9] The Italian's odd dress may be modelled on Mussolini's early liking for frock-coat and bowler-hat; see Mack Smith (*29*, p.106) and Bordeaux (*19*, p.219).

The suspiciously demonstrative quality in the Italians' current self-assertion emerges particularly clearly when the children try to ape their elders: 'Es gab Empfindlichkeiten, Äußerungen eines Selbstgefühls, das zu heikel und lehrhaft schien, um seinen Namen ganz zu verdienen' (pp.224f.). Conversely, the adults' response to Fuggiero's absurd 'Heldenjammergeschrei' not only confirms the narrator's general impression that there is a strong element of play-acting in the mood of the Italians, but also highlights two further, related features of their disposition. The first is their tendency to react as a crowd rather than as individuals; the second is their over-readiness to take seriously and to sympathize with the supposed suffering of one of their number. Yet, why should these people, who so evidently resent the way the 'others' impinge on their lives, be so ready to act in unison? As the name of 'Fuggiero'[10] suggests, the simple answer is cowardice: each individual, believing there is safety in numbers, wants to escape the threat posed by the crowds by becoming part of the crowd, thereby exchanging impotent individual frustration for the strength — and legitimized aggression — of the mass. Joining the fascist mob, in other words, is a way of counteracting a diminished sense of importance both on an individual and on a national level. Conversely, the explanation for the readiness of the crowd to identify with the injured bully is to be found in the feelings of weakness, injury and self-pity underlying the individual's assumption of a collective identity founded on discipline and the suppression of natural impulse.

---

[10] 'Fuggiero' is not a normal Italian name or word, but Mann presumably derived it from 'fuggire' (to flee).

4. The Magician

When Cipolla first emerges onto the platform to perform, his appearance is greeted by laughter in various parts of the hall. In the course of the evening, however, he succeeds in making virtually the whole audience do his bidding. How does he do it? What is there about this man which makes him into a leader of others? Compared with the bullish Mussolini, for example, he has none of the appearance of physical strength that helped the *Duce* convince people of his fitness to command. Quite the opposite, in fact, for Cipolla is a hunchback with an oddly awkward way of walking who wears clothes patently designed to conceal a physical disability. Indirectly, however, Cipolla's deformed body has just as much to do with his power over others as Mussolini's stocky frame. In this respect Mann's characterization of the tyrannical hypnotist owes as much to Friedrich Nietzsche's theory of power as to any historical model.

In the view of Nietzsche, the impulse to exercise power was *the* fundamental drive in life, although the forms in which it found expression were often devious and as varied as the multiplicity of human beings in whom it was at work. Originally, Nietzsche claimed, power lay in the hands of 'natural aristocrats' ('die Vornehmen'), men whom life had equipped with superior physical strength and courage (see 'Zur Genealogie der Moral' in *39*, Vol.2, pp.761-901). However, the dominance of the physically strong, born leaders did not remain unchallenged, because the will to power, present in all men, found new forms of expression in certain physically disadvantaged individuals who, subverting the 'natural' order of values, asserted the superiority of spiritual over physical strength. Hence the emergence in human societies of magicians, priests, moralists, artists, intellectuals, all of them bent on achieving some measure of power through the exercise of their particular gifts, and each

of them filled, to a greater or lesser extent, with feelings of
'Ressentiment' towards those whom nature had endowed more
generously with strength or beauty.[11]

In *Mario und der Zauberer* Cipolla concedes the facts of his
physical disability and poor health, but goes on to stress his
spiritual prowess and the recognition this has earned him:

> Mein Beruf ist schwer und meine Gesundheit nicht die
> robusteste; ich habe einen kleinen Leibesschaden zu
> beklagen, der mich außerstand gesetzt hat, am Kriege für
> die Größe des Vaterlandes teilzunehmen. Allein mit den
> Kräften meiner Seele und meines Geistes meistere ich das
> Leben, was ja immer nur heißt: sich selbst bemeistern, und
> schmeichle mir, mit meiner Arbeit die achtungsvolle
> Anteilnahme der gebildeten Öffentlichkeit erregt zu haben.
>
> (p.238)

Yet, while Cipolla, with his talk of 'sich selbst bemeistern', pays
lip-service to the Nietzschean virtue of 'Selbstüberwindung', his
behaviour tells another story. That he is far from having
overcome, by his spiritual achievements, a sense of inferiority
about his physical disability and ugliness, is made only too plain
by his inability to shrug off the challenge to his authority from
the handsome young Giovanotto (whose name connotes physical
robustness as well as youth):

> Jetzt hatte wieder der Bursche die Zeche zu zahlen, den
> Cipolla nicht müde wurde in der Rolle des donnaiuolo und
> ländlichen Hahnes im Korbe vorzuführen, — wobei die
> zähe Empfindlichkeit und Animosität, mit der er auf ihn
> zurückkam, in auffälligem Mißverhältnis zu den
> Äußerungen seines Selbstgefühles und zu den mondänen
> Erfolgen stand, deren er sich rühmte…es sprach aus seinen
> Spitzen doch auch echte Gehässigkeit, über deren
> menschlichen Sinn ein Blick auf die Körperlichkeit beider
> belehrt haben würde, auch wenn der Verwachsene nicht

[11] Mann's interpretation of Hitler in 'Ein Bruder' centres on the concept of
'Ressentiment' (*10*, Vol.2, p.223).

beständig auf das ohne weiteres vorausgesetzte Glück des hübschen Jungen bei den Frauen angespielt hätte. (p.239)

Cipolla's treatment of Giovanotto is part and parcel of his general misanthropy.[12] But it is more than this. Underlying Cipolla's air of arrogance are feelings of emotional vulnerability and sexual inadequacy. Occasionally these emotions show through the surface of self-confidence. For example, when the magician sits on the rigid body of one hypnotic subject in whom he has induced all the symptoms of cataleptic paralysis, he tells the audience, in words with overtones of blasphemy, that their sympathy should be directed at *him* rather than at his young victim, since it is really he who is having to suffer: 'Sono io, il poveretto! Ich bin es, der das alles duldet' (p.260). The narrator is taken aback by what seems to him an insolent and inappropriate demand for sympathy ('Beanspruchte er auch noch unser Mitgefühl? Wollte er alles haben?' p.259), yet what Cipolla is expressing vicariously here through the medium of his victim's rigid body, or when he makes Giovanotto seem to writhe with the pain of colic, is the helplessness and pain of a man who feels unloved and unlovable.

The same indirect, theatrical mode of expressing his hidden feelings is used by Cipolla on two further occasions, and each time his emotional needs become ever plainer. In the first incident he puts Signora Angiolieri into a hypnotic trance and leads her away, seemingly love-struck, from the side of her helpless husband. In his last, most grotesque 'Versuch'[13] of the evening Cipolla not only makes the hypnotized Mario believe that he is his beloved Silvestra, but even persuades this rejected lover to kiss him on the lips. There could be no clearer expression than this of Cipolla's desperate need for affection

[12] The misanthropy of both Mussolini and Goebbels was notorious. Like Cipolla, Goebbels particularly resented the success of other men with women (see Heiber, *23*, p.14).

[13] The word 'Versuch' is typical of the calculated ambiguities through which Mann introduces supernatural implications into an otherwise natural context. It means 'experiment' (as in science) but it also has alchemical associations with a suggestion of demoniacal temptation; 'versuchen' has the same ambiguity in *Doktor Faustus* (*9*, p.31).

which, because it is frustrated, becomes transformed into cruel mockery of others.[14] Although Cipolla's hypnotic illusions demonstrate the power of his will, they also reveal the underlying emotional weakness that seeks solace in illusion and compensation in tyranny.

---

[14] As Hatfield observes (*69*, p.309), the kiss also reveals a 'strong homosexual tendency' in Cipolla. This is another of Cipolla's 'Mephistophelian' characteristics (see below, pp.39f.).

5. *The Leader and the Led*

If the psychology of 'Ressentiment' helps to explain Cipolla's grim determination to impose his will on others, it remains to be explained why the others submit to his arrogant will. Simply to say that they are the victims of his skill as a hypnotist is not a sufficient explanation, for the success of hypnotic suggestion depends, it is generally accepted, on the subconscious assent of the hypnotic subject to what is being demanded of him. To understand the audience's acceptance of Cipolla's dominance, in other words, involves analysing the interaction of his behaviour with their complex and even contradictory psychological needs.

Cipolla's promise of an evening of entertainment lays the innocent-seeming basis of his power over the audience for it appeals to the Italians' love of theatre, and more particularly to their fondness for real-life drama. Just as the crowd on the beach readily formed an impromptu procession to accompany the 'wounded' Fuggiero, the audience assembled in the makeshift theatre of the *municipio* seems to the narrator to be eager not merely to watch events on the platform but also to slip into the adversarial roles assigned to them by Cipolla's provocative attitude:

> Man unterhielt sich bei dieser Art von Dramatik, obgleich sie den Eintritt ins eigentliche Programm mehr und mehr verzögerte. Einem Wortwechsel zuzuhören, ist immer fesselnd. Gewisse Menschen belustigt das einfach, und sie genießen aus einer Art von Schadenfreude ihr Nichtbeteiligtsein; andere empfinden Beklommenheit und Erregung, und ich verstehe sie sehr gut, wenn ich auch damals den Eindruck hatte, daß alles gewissermaßen auf Übereinkunft beruhte, und daß sowohl die beiden

analphabetischen Dickhäuter wie auch der Giovanotto in der Jacke dem Künstler halb und halb zur Hand gingen, um Theater zu produzieren. (pp.243f.)

Unfortunately, however, the traditional Italian taste for theatricality has become far from harmless in the prevailing social and political atmosphere, because it is now entangled with pressing psychological anxieties and tensions in the population. As we have seen, play-acting has become part of everyday life as the Italians lay claim to a collective persona that is at odds with an underlying sense of personal and national weakness: 'dies Publikum...prästierte Würde, *stellte* voreinander und vor dem Fremden Ernst und Haltung, wach aufgerichtete Ehrliebe *zur Schau*' [my italic] (p.224). Because the Italians at present do not have a strong, genuine sense of who they are, they are predisposed to accept a role assigned to them by someone else, particularly where that role is closely attuned to their underlying fears or desires.

One of the most important ways in which Cipolla exploits the uncertainties of his audience is by becoming an object of identification for them. Whereas the audience is made up of individuals whose bravado conceals inner weakness and uncertainty about their identity, Cipolla *appears* to be an embodiment of weakness turned into strength. Despite his extravagant clothing, he cannot hope to conceal for long the fact of his physical disadvantage, but nevertheless he faces the audience with seemingly impregnable self-assurance:

Das Publikum beobachtete ihn so scharf, wie es sich von ihm durchmustert sah. Bei den jungen Leuten auf den Stehplätzen sah man zusammengezogene Brauen und bohrende, nach einer Blöße spähende Blicke, die dieser allzu Sichere sich geben würde. Er gab sich keine. (p.235)

Although the 'Illusionista' Cipolla is in reality only acting a part, just as they are, he does so with sufficient conviction to persuade others that he truly is the man of iron will he wants them to take him for. Identification with this seeming strong-man (presumably the intended meaning of the odd term 'Forzatore', p.229) offers the members of the public a way of dealing with their own insecurity, for in him they see an embodiment of qualities they would like to possess and which they seek to share by identifying with him. In this, as in so many other details, the political and psychological astuteness of Mann's analysis of the relationship between the leader and the led is borne out by contemporary observers of Mussolini and the findings of his biographers. Laura Fermi, for example, argues that the cohesive force in Italian fascist society was 'not Mussolini the man, but Mussolini the myth, in which his followers wanted to believe' (*22*, p.193), a view confirmed by the dramatist Pirandello who is said to have recognized in the *Duce* 'essentially an actor pretending to be the person the Italians wanted him to be' (see *29*, p.112). J.P. Stern has applied the same argument to the case of Hitler (*32*, p.16).

As well as strength of will, Cipolla's behaviour exhibits aggressiveness, a trait which is certainly resented, at a conscious level at least, by the audience. Although this might seem to create an obstacle to their willingness to identify with him, his provocations actually contribute to that process by exploiting the masochistic inclinations of the audience. Cipolla's method is first to excite the audience's aggressions by his arrogant scorn of them, and then to confront them with his hypnotic eyes and the whistling menace of his whip, to which even the narrator finds himself submitting involuntarily from the very outset: 'ich erinnere mich, daß ich unwillkürlich mit den Lippen leise das Geräusch nachahmte, mit dem Cipolla seine Reitpeitsche hatte durch die Luft fahren lassen' (p.237). The cowardice of the spectators frustrates the outward ventilation of their aggressions on Cipolla, so that these are forced back on the members of the audience themselves. Cipolla's power, in other words, derives from his victims' own emotional tendencies which simply gain freer, more marked expression under his influence. In order to bring about their identification with *his* will, Cipolla merely has to activate the same psychological mechanisms through which his victims have already sublimated their individual aggressions into submissive identification with the 'Will of Italy' and transferred their sense of individual selfhood to the collective.

The resentment involved in that transfer only tightens the bonds binding them to their 'Bändiger' (p.261), for the treatment they accept from him is a form of self-punishment for acquiescing in the new, ascetic, fascist way of life which, privately, each individual deeply dislikes. The hypnotist's first experiment with the rebellious Giovanotto symbolizes this sado-masochistic complex. When Giovanotto sticks out his tongue at the audience, the aggression he feels towards Cipolla is redirected both towards himself (in his self-humiliation) and against those in whose name he first challenged Cipolla. Giovanotto's insulting behaviour thus expresses, on the one hand, the individual's hostility towards the mass of the others, and, on the other, self-hatred for submitting first to the collective and now to Cipolla. Although Giovanotto's behaviour superficially shocks the audience, he is in fact acting out their own unadmitted emotional tensions. By the end of the evening they all will be giving equal affront to their own standards of respectability as they dance to the mocking swish of Cipolla's whip — enjoying the compensation for habitual self-denial which he facilitates, and simultaneously punishing themselves both for needing and for accepting such compensation.

The third psychological component in Cipolla's control of the crowd is the feeling of release that identification with him offers from the conflict between the desire to maintain one's independence as an individual and the pressures of the collective. To become one of the herd ruled by Cipolla's 'Stab der Kirke' (p.266)[15] is to flee temporarily from the tensions of selfhood into irresponsible anonymity. As he describes the dance which marks the apogee of Cipolla's power, Mann again illustrates generally felt emotions by concentrating on an individual case, in this instance a gentleman from Rome who is determined to disobey Cipolla's command to dance. Gradually the man's resistance weakens and the narrator observes, with a

[15] In *The Odyssey* Circe was a sorceress who could turn men into swine; see the essay by Martin (*80*).

mixture of horror and eventual relief, a smile of pleasure spreading over the man's face as this champion of human dignity surrenders his will, exchanging the strenuousness of maintaining his personal independence for the relaxation of submission to the general atmosphere of self-abandonment:

> So war es, das Zucken und Zerren im Körper des Widerspenstigen nahm überhand, er hob die Arme, die Knie, auf einmal lösten sich alle seine Gelenke, er warf die Glieder, er tanzte, und so führte der Cavaliere ihn, während die Leute klatschten, aufs Podium, um ihn den anderen Hampelmännern anzureihen. Man sah nun das Gesicht des Unterworfenen, es war dort oben veröffentlicht. Er lächelte breit, mit halbgeschlossenen Augen, während er sich 'vergnügte'. Es war eine Art von Trost, zu sehen, daß ihm offenbar wohler war jetzt als zur Zeit seines Stolzes...
> (pp.265f.)

Finally, Cipolla's power is shown to derive from the quality of the emotions he enables the crowd to experience. Both when he sticks out his tongue at the others and when he abandons himself in public to the seeming agony of a colic, Giovanotto's behaviour may be said to be regressive, more like that of a young child than a grown man (see Böhme, *58*, p.309). In yielding to the hypnotist's will, in other words, Giovanotto and the others are able to lose the inhibitions which civilized conduct demands. Mann therefore links such regression to childish behaviour with regression to primitive behaviour. Thus the drunkenly dancing audience is described like some tribe moving to the rhythm of its witch-doctor's stick, rather as Mann was later to characterize crowd behaviour at political rallies: 'Neulich sah ich im Film einen Sakraltanz von Bali-Insulanern, der in vollkommener Trance und schrecklichen Zuckungen der erschöpften Jünglinge endete. Wo ist der Unterschied zwischen diesen Bräuchen und den Vorgängen in einer politischen Massenversammlung Europas?' (*10*, Vol.2, p.225).

The seduction of regressing to pre-rational forms of behaviour was, Thomas Mann believed, an important reason for the success of the fascists in 'aestheticizing politics' (the phrase is Walter Benjamin's). Fascism both appealed to 'archaic' layers of the personality, exploiting primitive emotions at carefully orchestrated mass meetings by means of ritualized chanting and gesture, and promised, falsely, a lasting escape from the social and psychological complexities of modern existence into the supposed simplicity of earlier times when the leader led and the led, unquestioning, followed. Again, however, the events of Cipolla's evening do not mirror events in the political domain in a simple or direct way. Although the meaning of Hitler's or Mussolini's treatment of their audiences may have been humiliation, this message was not conveyed by the surface symbolism of their rallies. These demagogues did not parade their scorn of the masses openly and provocatively, but flattered them as members of great nations woefully wronged by the rest of Europe. Mann's story could only convey what he believed lay beneath that surface of flattery by studying the psychological mechanisms of tyranny under the specially intensified ('gesteigert'), experimental conditions of fiction.[16]

---

[16] Mann used Goethe's concept of 'Steigerung' to refer to the heightening of reality through art.

6. Myth

The behaviour of the entranced crowd dancing around Cipolla is not only generally reminiscent of primitive rituals but has quite particular cultural associations within the context of German literature. Again, the work of Friedrich Nietzsche, and in particular his widely influential study, *The Birth of Tragedy from the Spirit of Music* (in *39*, Vol.1, pp.7-135), was one of the main sources to which Mann turned for help with the task of interpreting his experiences in fascist Italy to a German readership in terms with which they would be familiar.

The origins of Greek tragedy, Nietzsche had argued, were to be sought in the rites of a god known to the Greeks as Dionysos, and to the ancient Romans as Bacchus. The worship of this divinity, he claimed, had spread to Greece from the East via Asia Minor. This cult was originally part of a widespread pattern of pagan nature-worship ('rites of spring'), but the unique achievement of the Greeks was to transform the worship of Dionysos from a wild, animalistic, intoxicated orgy of sexuality and blood-letting into an artistic, symbolic celebration of the creative forces and processes in the world. The rudimentary artistic germ from which tragedy grew was a chanting, dancing chorus of worshippers who, in a state of emotional intoxication or 'Rausch', imagined themselves to be 'satyrs' — mythical creatures, half human, half animal in appearance — attending at the death and rebirth of their satyr-god Dionysos.

The magician Cipolla is a late reincarnation of the Dionysian. This explains, for example, the odd nature of his physical deformity: the unusual location of his 'hump' at the *base* of his spine (rather than between the shoulders) gives Cipolla a profile that recalls the 'kinked' shape of the satyr whose human torso emerged from the hindquarters of a goat. Hence, too, the

explicity drunken quality of the dance Cipolla induces (an
allusion to the 'Rausch' of the Dionysian worshippers), and the
description of the dance as an irresistible, impersonal force that
seizes the individual's body:

> So war es, das Zucken und Zerren im Körper des
> Widerspenstigen nahm überhand, er hob die Arme, die
> Knie, auf einmal lösten sich alle seine Gelenke, er warf die
> Glieder, er tanzte (p.265)

Yet it may be objected, quite properly, that Cipolla's frequently
flagging 'Zappelkorps' (p.271) is a pale shadow of the
enthusiastic celebrants of primal energy conjured up in the *Birth
of Tragedy*. Equally, the 'Herr des Abends' has himself
repeatedly to use *artificial* stimulants, tobacco and spirits, to
induce in his own person the 'Rausch' he needs to drive himself
on despite his easily exhausted mental and physical energies.
Clearly, what the narrator witnesses in Torre di Venere is not so
much a renewal of the ancient Dionysian spirit as a travesty of it
— Dionysos 'auf der Stufe der Verhunzung', as Müller-Salget
(echoing Nietzsche's verdict on the hypnotic art of Wagner)
aptly puts it (*86*, p.61).

In the social and psychological conditions prevailing in Torre
di Venere the re-emergence of myth is thus characterized as a
process of dissolution into emotional and mental anarchy: 'eine
gewisse Ausartung, ein gewisses spätnächtliches Drunter und
Drüber der Gemüter, eine trunkene Auflösung der kritischen
Widerstände' (p.263). As they unconsciously re-enact mythical
roles, Cipolla and his audience exhibit weakness rather than
vigour, the breakdown of their culture rather than the kind of
rejuvenation promised by Mussolini's exaltation of the mythical
greatness of Rome, and paralleled in Germany by the Nazis' cult
of Nordic myths — most notably in Rosenberg's *Der Mythus des
zwanzigsten Jahrhunderts* (*40*). Whereas the vitality of the early
Greeks had enabled them to draw creative stimulus from the
tension between the opposing forces of order and raw energy,
the members of Cipolla's audience, exhausted by the conflicts of
modern civilization, simply allow themselves to be pitched from

one extreme of excessive self-discipline to the opposite extreme of utter self-abandonment. As it dances drunkenly under Cipolla's whip, the audience presents an image of brutality combined with anarchy, a combination that, in Nietzschean terms, is quintessentially decadent. It may well be that the 'tragisches Reiseerlebnis' mentioned in the sub-title of the story refers to the narrator's experience of witnessing the terrible decay that has befallen a once great and creative civilization.[17]

In addition to these Dionysian overtones, Mann's magician has another mythological dimension, one that would have been even plainer to his German readership. Cipolla is a literary descendant of the devil, or, to be more precise, of Mephistopheles, as the devil is known in Goethe's *Faust*. This connection is suggested not only by the many words or phrases suggesting that his hypnotic powers have a supernatural quality, expressions such as 'ungeheuerlich', 'Nicht-Geheuerlichkeit', 'unheimlich', 'Dämonie', 'Behexung', 'niedrige Form der Offenbarung', but also by many features of Cipolla's appearance and behaviour. His self-designation as 'Cavaliere Cipolla' (p.233), for example, echoes Mephisto's words of introduction, 'Ich bin ein Kavalier, wie andere Kavaliere' (*37*, line 2511). Not only does Cipolla's impeded gait recall that of Mephisto ('Der Ritter mit dem Pferdefuß', *37*, line 4141), but his hair, swept forward at the temples, has a faint suggestion of the devil's horns: 'während das Schläfenhaar, ebenfalls geschwärzt, seitlich zu den Augenwinkeln hingestrichen war' (p.240). Like Mephisto, Cipolla is a master of barbed wit, while the entirely negative uses to which he puts his spiritual powers accord with Mephisto's famous description of his role in life: 'Ich bin der Geist, der stets verneint' (*37*, line 1338). Just as Mephisto conjured up a vision of Gretchen in order to seduce Faust, so Cipolla has the ability to make his last victim, the waiter Mario, believe he can see his beloved Silvestra. Similarly, Mephisto's use of his power of illusion to deceive the whole crowd of revellers in 'Auerbachs Keller' is imitated by Cipolla's

[17] Cf Mann's remarks about Germany after the Nazi 'Machtergreifung' in 1933: 'Die Tragik des heutigen Deutschlands ist die Tragik eines früher erhabenen Landes, das sich jetzt vor den Augen der Welt erniedrigt' (*11*, p.199).

use of the same power to master his audience in the *municipio*.
As Mephisto has traditionally taken Faust on magical journeys
to fabulous places, so Cipolla 'transports' an elderly lady to
India and makes Signora Angiolieri willing to 'schweben' with
him 'bis ans Ende der Welt' (p.262).

There is a connection too between the dance conducted by
Cipolla in Torre di Venere and the orgiastic dance to which
Mephisto leads Faust on the Brocken (Goethe's Germanic name
for the Venusberg of legend). Cipolla's ever ready and never
failing 'Benzinfeuerzeug' recalls Mephisto's trick of snapping
fire from his fingers, while the repeated references to his
exhaling streams of smoke through his sharp and ugly teeth are a
reminder that Mephistopheles is 'vor allem Herr des *Feuers*, das
er sich als das zerstörend-keimlose, keimwidrige Element
vorbehalten hat' (*2*, p.671). It also seems quite likely that
Mann's last description of the dead Cipolla ('reglos,
ein durcheinandergeworfenes Bündel Kleider und schiefer
Knochen', p.275) was intended by Mann as an allusion to the
puppet-play through which Goethe first became familiar with
the Faust legend. This allusion is then reinforced by the pattern
of poetic justice in the story, for, having been the demonic
puppet-master arrogantly and gleefully manipulating his crowd
of 'Hampelmännern' (p.266), Cipolla himself collapses in a
heap on the stage like some abandoned marionette.

Mann's association of Cipolla with two mythological
traditions, the Dionysian and the satanic, contributes in various
ways to the overall meaning of the story. Firstly, the link with
Mephisto gives the story greater moral clarity than is often to be
found in Mann's fiction. Although Cipolla is one of those
'Nietzschean' characters in whom extraordinary spiritual gifts
are released through the agency of sickness and disability, his
use of those abilities is defined as entirely destructive, perverse
and diabolical.

Secondly, the satanic overtones enlarge the scope of what is
implied by the figure of the 'Scharlatan' and 'illusionista'.
Cipolla is repeatedly and variously associated with deception
and falsity. Having delayed his appearance, for example, he
walks onto the platform very rapidly to create the 'Täuschung'

or 'Fiktion' (p.233) of having hurried a long way to reach the theatre. His dyed hair and the cut of his clothes ('hier falsch gestrafft und dort in falschen Falten', p.234) are likewise designed to deceive. The narrator suspects that his sash, assumed by others to be 'das Abzeichen des Cavaliere', is simply 'reiner Humbug' (p.235). After observing his first so-called 'Zauberkunststücke', the narrator is convinced, 'daß der Mann unter falscher Flagge segelte; nur welches seine richtige war, blieb undeutlich' (p.241). As his essay on Goethe's *Faust* makes clear, falsity of this kind was for Thomas Mann a fundamental, perhaps even *the* essential quality of the satanic: 'si diabolus non esset mendax et homicida' are words Adrian Leverkühn, hero of *Doktor Faustus*, has to hear repeatedly. The devil's whole existence is mendacious in the sense that, as the negation of human and divine love, he holds up a distorting mirror to life, making it *seem* a realm of hatred and ugliness. Ultimately, Cipolla's power, like that of the Antichrist or 'Tyrant of the Last Days', is founded on illusion.

Finally, Cipolla's association with Mephistopheles helps to define the scope as well as the nature of the evil embodied in the magician. In his essay on Goethe's *Faust* Mann elaborates with evident sympathy on Goethe's treatment of evil as a parasitic, subordinate force whose negativity unwittingly performs an ultimately useful service within the wider scheme of things, 'Ein Teil von jener Kraft, die stets das Böse will und stets das Gute schafft' (*37*, line 1335). The imagery of disease in *Mario und der Zauberer* implies something similar about Mann's own Cipolla-Mephisto. The positive role of this psychologically disturbed figure is to bring to a head the moral and social 'Krankheit' that is affecting the crowds in Torre di Venere and, by embodying and externalizing the destructive potential of that disease, to summon up the instinctive resistance of healthy forces to the threat he represents. In a phrase Mann used to describe Hitler and his relationship to the German people, Cipolla is 'der Exzedent des Unbewußten' (*10*, Vol.2, p.226), an emanation of the collective unconscious and, as such, a figure whose power really derives from the psychological needs of those whom he leads. Hence, again, the aptness of his final transformation

from puppeteer into marionette, discarded and lifeless now that
he has fulfilled his function of embodying the (now exorcized)
evil impulses of his ostensible victims.

7. Culture and Politics

Mann's incorporation of satanic and Dionysian myths in a story so clearly concerned with the political dangers facing contemporary Europe may strike the English reader as a little odd. Partly, this can be explained by his general belief that myths describe certain patterns in human behaviour which recur throughout history. As he worked on the novel *Joseph und seine Brüder* during the late 1920s, however, he had become increasingly aware both of the variety of myths and of the different ways they could be interpreted and used. The hero of that novel, Joseph, has a keen sense of self-interest which shapes his understanding and (ironic) execution of his mythically 'preordained' role in life. Conversely, under the influence of Freud, Mann had come to understand that the rigid repetition of archetypal patterns was a symptom of neurotic compulsion ('Wiederholungszwang'), which could only be broken by men acquiring insight into their own motives. These reflections had acquired a particular focus during the 1920s, a period when myth and the interpretation of myth occupied an important position in cultural-political debate. The role of myth in *Mario und der Zauberer* becomes clearer if seen in relation to those debates.

As the author of the *Betrachtungen eines Unpolitischen*, in which he had explained and justified Germany's involvement in the First World War in terms of his countrymen's attachment to a culture founded on the values of a supposedly apolitical, Romantic 'inwardness' ('Innerlichkeit'), Thomas Mann was well placed to understand the threat that was posed to the establishment of democracy in the Weimar Republic by the Germans' continuing attachment to that cultural tradition, since it associated democracy with rationalistic materialism and with the 'alien' value-system of the 'old enemy', France.

Conservative opponents of the young Weimar Republic (to
which Mann began to lend his support in public in 1922)
denounced the Republic (and the Treaty of Versailles that had
called it into being) as a wholly 'un-German' creation which had
been brutally imposed on Germany by the victorious Entente
powers in an attempt to cut the country off from its cultural
roots. In these polemics 'myth' was regularly used as an emotive
code-word to imply rejection of 'modern' or 'Western'
rationalism and its political expression, the 'shallow',
'calculating' system of parliamentary democracy. Having
learned from his own experiences that 'in jeder geistigen
Haltung ist das Politische latent' (*10*, Vol.3, p.161), and that,
particularly in Germany, 'zwischen Kuturpolitik und
eigentlicher Politik keine Grenze mehr haltbar ist' (*10*, Vol.2,
p.100), Thomas Mann set himself the task of exposing the
hidden political agenda implicit in the reactionary interpretations
of myth current at the time, and of proposing another view of
myth, one informed by Freud's psycho-analytic insights and
hence capable of contributing to human progress.

As an inhabitant of Munich, Mann not only had the head-
quarters of the Nazi movement on his doorstep but also various
cultural expressions of the increasingly reactionary atmosphere
in that city, including the 'Münchner Kreis', a group of right-
wing intellectuals led by Ludwig Klages whose notorious *Der
Geist als Widersacher der Seele* was a sustained attack on the
faculty of reason, 'Geist', because it had supposedly cut modern
man off from the deeper, irrational layers of his imagination or
soul, 'Seele', and thus denied him access to the symbolic and
mythical intuitions of life's true meaning with which men living
in ancient cultures had once been blessed. When Alfred
Bäumler, another member of the circle, published a new edition
of J.J. Bachofen's *Der Mythus von Occident und Orient* Mann
seized the opportunity to launch an invective of his own against
the enfeebled versions of Romantic thought circulating in the
present.[18] In particular he denounced the accompanying claim
that the way into the future necessitated a return to the past,

[18] As Dierks has shown (*44*, pp.172-77), Mann's criticism of Bäumler actually
sprang from misunderstanding in this instance.

declaring this to be, 'eine Fiktion voller Tagestendenz, bei welcher es sich nicht sowohl um den Geist von Heidelberg als um den von München handelt'.[19]

Mann's anger at the obscurantist ideology being peddled by Klages and his like was channelled into *Mario und der Zauberer* by building into the complex, composite figure of Cipolla a satirical portrait of the intellectual as an aider and abetter of the politics of reaction. Cipolla's subservient relationship to the *Duce* in Rome, taken together with his heady allusions to determinist thinking casts him in the role of the intellectual supporter of fascism. Cipolla's concentration on the youth in his audience and his praise of the fatherland's greatness as he stands before the blackboard word carry a strong suggestion of the 'professoraler Chauvinismus' (*6*, p.437) in the Weimar Republic which affected even men like Ernst Bertram whom Mann had long known and respected.

Of course, although intellectuals like those associated with the 'Munich circle' contributed to the general 'Verwirrung' of thought and values in which fascism could be made to seem a respectable political creed, Cipolla works much more directly and magnetically on the public than such men ever could. In this respect the figure of the hypnotist is reminiscent of another arch-romantic 'Hexenmeister' whose power over audiences the Nazis were keen to enlist in the service of their own cause, namely Richard Wagner. Like the narrator's attitude to Cipolla, Mann's response to Wagner was complicated and ambivalent. He was fascinated and often deeply moved by Wagner's musical and imaginative gifts, but he had come to sympathize increasingly with Nietzsche's critique of the seductive, decadent romanticism in Wagner's work. On the one hand he poured scorn on the attempts by the German reactionaries to assimilate Wagner's sophisticated mythical dramas to their own simple-minded 'Wotanskult':

[19] Heidelberg was one of the centres of Romanticism. Munich, in Mann's view, had become not only the home of Nazism but of a more general cultural and political reaction in the 1920s.

Zu denken, daß Wagner noch heute, bei den
Restaurationsversuchen Bayreuths, als Schutzherr einer
höhlenbärenmäßigen Deutschtümelei und Vertreter roher
Biederkeit mißbraucht werden kann. (*18*, p.246)

Yet on the other hand, Mann recognized that Wagner's
Dionysian art appealed so powerfully to certain feelings
(fatalism, a love of grandeur, the seduction of death) that it lent
itself all too easily to just such conservative or even fascist
misuse: 'Es sind *reaktionäre* Züge in Wagners Erscheinung,
Züge von Rückwärtsgewandtheit und dunklem Vergangen-
heitskult' (*10*, Vol.3, p.113).

Certain details in the characterization of Cipolla suggest that
one of Mann's aims was to caricature precisely these
'reaktionäre Züge in Wagners Erscheinung'. The curious
observation, for example, that, 'Vielleicht mehr als irgendwo ist
in Italien das achtzehnte Jahrhundert noch lebendig und mit
ihm der Typus des Scharlatans, des marktschreierischen
Possenreißers' (p.233) echoes both Gottfried Keller's famous
denunciation of Wagner as a 'Friseur und Charlatan' and
Nietzsche's comparison of Wagner to Cagliostro (*9*, Vol.2,
p.913). The fact that Cipolla appears attired in a 'weiten
schwarzen und ärmellosen Radmantel mit Samtkragen und
atlasgefütterter Pelerine' (p.233) recalls Wagner's notoriously
theatrical taste in clothes and, more specifically, his love of
'*Atlas*schlafröcke' and '*Samt* und Seide' [my italic] (*10*, Vol.3,
p.102). Similarly, Wagner's highly-strung disposition, which
meant that he could only work in short, intense spurts ('im
Kampf mit einer jedesmal rasch erschöpften Kraft', ibid., p.84)
is paralleled by Cipolla's fragile health ('meine Gesundheit nicht
die robusteste', p.238) and his need for artificial stimulants to
counteract exhaustion ('zur Erhaltung und Erneuerung seiner
Spannkraft', p.251). Perhaps more important than any of these
details, however, is Mann's portrayal of Cipolla as the type of
artist for whom art is a means of achieving power. Mann's
comment on the link between Wagner and Bismarck is relevant
to that between Cipolla and Mussolini:

Wagner war Politiker genug, seine Sache mit der des
Bismarck'schen Reiches zu verbinden: er sah einen Erfolg
ohnegleichen, er schloß den seinen daran, und die
europäische Hegemonie seiner Kunst ist das kulturelle
Zubehör zur politischen Hegemonie Bismarcks geworden.

(*10*, Vol.3, p.l09)

Such satirical barbs represent only one side of Mann's view of
Wagner whose work he valued for, amongst other things, its
affinity with Freud's analysis of neurosis — a form of praise
calculated to infuriate Wagner's Nazi following. In *Mario*,
however, Mann's pen was guided principally by his concern
about the politically suspect aspects of an art as powerfully
seductive and hypnotic as Wagner's.

8. The Problem of Freedom

At the time of writing *Mario und der Zauberer* Thomas Mann was deeply preoccupied with the question of human freedom. His essays and lectures on Heine (1927), Fontane (1928), Freud (1929), Lessing (1929) and Goethe (1932) all lay similar stress on the importance of critical, intellectual and moral freedom as an enduring and central component in the German cultural tradition and as a counterwieght to Romantic-irrationalist elements in that tradition.

But equally, Mann was acutely aware both of how problematic a concept freedom is, and of how powerful the social and psychological constraints on it are. At the beginning of the twenties, in an essay on 'Goethe und Tolstoi', he had asked himself whether liberalism might not already have to be considered a thing of the past:

> Europa scheint diese Frage bereits beantwortet zu haben. *Der anti-liberale Rückschlag ist mehr als klar*, er ist kraß. Er äußert sich politisch in der *überdrußvollen Abkehr von Demokratie und Parlamentarismus*, in einer mit finsteren Brauen vollzogenen Wendung *zur Diktatur und zum Terror*. Der Faschismus Italiens ist das genaue Gegenstück zum russischen Bolschewismus. (*18*, pp.213f.)

By the early 1930s Mann was forced to the conclusion that the very same mass-psychological forces which had driven freedom out of public life in Russia and Italy were now having the same effect in Germany:

> Die Welt wird sich an einen Zustand Deutschlands gewöhnen müssen, der, als eine deutsche, unheimlich

eigentümliche und eigensinnige Erscheinung weltpsycho-
logischer Prozesse, dem Zustand Rußlands u. Italiens
entspricht. (*15*, p.42)

As Mann saw it, freedom was threatened not simply by such
external constraints as the use of force to achieve political ends
but also by the possibility that men might actually prefer to live
without freedom:

Nichts ist naiver, als die Freiheit fröhlich moralisierend
gegen den Despotismus auszuspielen, denn sie ist ein
beängstigendes Problem, beängstigend in dem Maße, daß
es sich fragt, ob der Mensch um seiner seelischen und
metaphysischen Geborgenheit willen nicht lieber den
Schrecken will als die Freiheit. (*12*, p.29)

The success of anti-democratic, anti-liberal movements, whether
they be of the radical Left (Bolshevism) or of the radical Right
(fascism), rested, Mann feared, on the fact that they provided
men with a means of escaping the challenges of a life founded on
individual freedom and responsibility:

Das Kollektive ist bequeme Sphäre im Vergleich mit dem
Individuellen, bequem bis zur Liederlichkeit; was das
kollektivistische Geschlecht sich wünscht, sich gönnt und
bewilligt, sind die immerwährenden Ferien vom Ich...Der
Zweck, auf den es ankommt, ist der Rausch, die Befreiung
vom Ich, vom Denken, genaugenommen vom Sittlichen
und Vernünftigen überhaupt; auch von der *Angst*
natürlich, der Lebensangst, die dazu drängt, sich kollektiv-
istisch zusammenzudrücken, es menschenwarm zu haben
und recht laut zu singen. (*10*, Vol.2, pp.163f.)

The popularity in the 1920s of *Der Untergang des Abendlandes*
by Oswald Spengler, whom Mann denounced as a 'Defaitist der
Humanität' (*10*, Vol.3, p.148) for the way he seemed to relish
the 'iron inevitability' of history, struck Mann as a worrying
sign of the times.

Mann's deeply troubled awareness of the difficulties involved in asserting human freedom permeates *Mario und der Zauberer*. At the end the reader is left to ponder the narrator's paradoxical reflection that Mario's shooting of Cipolla was, 'Ein Ende mit Schrecken, ein höchst fatales Ende. Und ein befreiendes dennoch, — ich konnte und kann nicht umhin, es so zu empfinden!' (p.275). The narrator feels liberated by the catastrophe, but at the same time he describes it as 'fatal', an epithet connoting not just deadliness but also fatefulness or fatedness. As such, the term forms the last link in a chain of fate-motifs running through the story. Thus in the opening paragraph the motif of fate is sounded twice, first in the statement that the brooding evil in Torre di Venere was concentrated in the person of Cipolla 'auf *verhängnishafte*...Weise' [my italic] (p.215), and then in a pointer to the coming catastrophe: 'dem Ende mit Schrecken (einem, wie uns nachträglich schien, *vorgezeichneten* und im Wesen der Dinge liegenden Ende)' [my italic] (p.215). The chain continues in references to 'diesen fatalen Cipolla' (p.227), in the observation that Cipolla's hypnotic powers prove to be a 'Verhängnis' (p.256) as much for himself as for others, and in the description of Mario's stubby pistol as having been pointed in Cipolla's direction by fate: 'deren fast nicht vorhandenen Lauf das Schicksal in so unvorhergesehene und fremde Richtung gelenkt hatte' (p.275). The adjective 'unvorhergesehen' in this last passage did not appear in the first published version of the story (see *16*, p.136). The effect of its subsequent insertion was to emphasize still more firmly the role of fate rather than human volition in determining the outcome. Seen in relation to these motifs, the curiously circumlocutory description of Mario's weapon as 'die kleine, stumpfmetallne, kaum pistolenförmige Maschinerie' (p.275) similarly adds to the impression that events are dictated by the operation of some impersonal mechanism.

Not only does the narrator use the vocabulary of fate, but what he describes repeatedly exemplifies the loss of human freedom. Thus, although Giovanotto declares that he will not stick out his tongue at the magician's behest, he is unable to assert the freedom of his will in practice. This pattern of challenge and defeat recurs again and again, culminating in Cipolla's protracted tussle of wills with the 'Herrn aus Rom' which ends, as did all the others, with the magician's humiliating triumph over even the most determined, heroic efforts to defend 'die Ehre des Menschengeschlechts' (p.264).

Those critics who are least sympathetic towards the narrator see a damning parallel between the inability of the gentleman from Rome to assert the freedom of his will against Cipolla and the narrator's acceptance of Cipolla's commentary on events.[20] Although the narrator at first expresses his reservations about the magician's confusing attacks on freedom ('Man mußte zugeben, daß er seine Worte nicht besser hätte wählen können, um die Wasser zu trüben und seelische Verwirrung anzurichten', p.251), he later concedes that Cipolla's view seems in fact to be borne out by the failure of another of his victims to resist his power:

> Was für ein konfuser Vorgang! Er schien zu wollen und nicht zu können; aber er konnte wohl nur nicht wollen, und es waltete da jene die Freiheit lähmende Verstrickung des Willens in sich selbst, die unser Bändiger vorhin schon dem römischen Herrn höhnisch vorausgesagt hatte. (p.261)

Yet if Cipolla's deterministic view of behaviour appears to be confirmed both by the narrator and by the evidence of the events, what is one to make of the narrator's sense of liberation at the end of the story? Is *Mario und der Zauberer* in fact a tacit confession on Mann's part that the assertions of human freedom and dignity in his speeches and essays were empty rhetoric, mere wishful thinking? Or is there some way of differentiating between Cipolla's mocking denials of freedom of choice to his victims and the explanation of events offered by the story as a whole, and thus of reconciling the narrator's sense of liberation at the end with the chain of causation that runs through the story?

[20] Cf Gray (*66*, p.178) and Böhme (*58*, p.299); Böhme's arguments have been countered by Dierks (*60*, p.178), while Müller-Salget has rightly stressed the historically determined nature of the loss of freedom in the story (*86*, p.65).

Firstly it is important to recognize that the allusions to
Schopenhauer in the story are mainly to his essay on hypnotism
or 'animalischer Magnetismus', as it was known at the time.[21]
Schopenhauer's belief that the 'Wesen der Dinge' is a universal
Will through which the hypnotist or 'Magnetiseur' commun-
icates his wishes to the hypnotic subject clearly underlies the
account given in the story of Cipolla's manipulation of the
audience:

> ...die auf über- oder untervernünftigen Fähigkeiten der
> menschlichen Natur, auf Intuition und 'magnetischer'
> Übertragung, kurzum auf einer niedrigen Form der
> Offenbarung beruhen...diesem blinden Ausführen
> zusammengesetzter Handlungen, zu dem die Anweisung
> auf unerforschtem Wege, von Organismus zu Organismus
> ergeht (p.252)

In particular, Schopenhauer's commentary on the magical
power of 'fascination', or 'evil eye', whereby a sorcerer could
lay hold of and bind the will of a victim, is reflected not only in
the 'Faszination' (p.257)[22] exercised by Cipolla over his whole
audience but also in those 'Versuche' in which he 'lähmt' and
'krümmt' individual victims (see *41*, p.117). Cipolla's
demonstration of the interchangeability of 'Befehlen' and
'Gehorchen' similarly illustrates the existence of 'einen stummen
in der Luft liegenden Gemeinschaftswillen' (p.253); whether he
appears to command or to obey, the magician is simply using his
special understanding of the hidden impulses of the Will in
which all creatures participate.

What all these experiments demonstrate, however, is not the
universally determined character of existence which rules out
any freedom of action but the particular restriction of freedom
produced by the influence of hypnotism. Once that restriction is

[21] Schopenhauer's essay on 'animal magnetism' is contained in *41*, Vol.4,
pp.99-127.

[22] 'Faszination' is linked etymologically to 'fascism', both words being
concerned with forms of binding; cf the related pun on the 'fascinarii' in *Doktor
Faustus* (*9*, p.359).

lifted, Cipolla's victims are free again to distinguish illusion from truth and to act as they see fit — as Mario does, much to the astonishment of the arrogant Cipolla (although Cipolla's own *unconscious* will has been moving towards this end all along).

This brings us to the second major consideration Mann brings to bear on the question of freedom in the story, namely the role of pathology or 'Krankheit' in limiting human freedom. In this connection, another of the slight but important revisions he made between the first published version of the story and its later publication in book form is instructive. In the first version the narrator tells his children, puzzled by the hostile atmosphere in Torre, that the Italians are suffering from 'etwas wie eine Krankheit' (*16*, p.117); in the definitive version of the story this explanation has been expanded by a significant detail: 'etwas wie eine Krankheit, wenn sie wollten, nicht sehr angenehm, aber wohl notwendig' (p.225). Through this insertion of the word 'notwendig' Mann linked the concept of illness to that of 'necessity' in an ambiguous way which linked the idea of psychological compulsion to that of moral necessity.

When Mann referred to 'disease' in public life (as he frequently did during the 1920s), he was not just describing a moral problem in metaphorical terms, but was following Freud's analysis of neurosis as a compulsive type of behaviour that could manifest itself in collective as well as individual forms. In the 'restorative', backward-looking tendencies in Weimar Germany, for example, he recognized classic symptoms of neurotic repression ('Verdrängung'):

> Die Zeit, der vor sich selber graut, ist voll von Restaur-
> ationsverlangen...Umsonst, es gibt kein Züruck. Alle
> Flucht in lebensleer gewordene historische Formen ist
> Obskurantismus; alles fromme 'Verdrängen' der
> Erkenntnis schafft nur Lüge und Krankheit. (*8*, p.183)

In Mann's view, the Germans' pathological refusal to acknowledge the catastrophic 'physischen und psychischen Kollapsus' (*18*, p.217) of 1918 was bound to produce a fateful,

compulsive form of behaviour whereby people kept repeating
the same painful and self-injuring pattern of historical
experience. Instead Mann wanted his countrymen to analyse the
causes of the war and to use that terrible experience to grow in
self-knowledge. He wanted them to understand the war, and the
fatal 'Rausch' it inspired, in terms of historical, social *and* moral
necessity: 'eine historische *Notwendigkeit*, "um Europa auf eine
neue Stufe seiner sozialen Bildung zu heben"' [my italic] (*6*,
p.524); 'die germanische Neigung zum Rausch, zur Trunkenheit
...Vielleicht ist das eine Krankheit, die man gehabt haben *muß*,
um heute in Dingen des Lebens mitreden zu dürfen' [my italic]
(*18*, p.234).

The 'Krankheit' that is rampant in Torre di Venere is
'notwendig' in just this double sense. It is a historically, socially
and psychologically determined, pathological condition which,
like any illness, must run its course to its 'vorgezeichneten
Ende'. Cipolla's mocking demonstration of his victims' lack of
freedom is made possible by the fact that they are at present in
the grip of neurotic, sado-masochistic compulsions which make
them susceptible to his hypnotic suggestion and manipulation.
At the same time this humiliating experience is also 'wohl
notwendig' in a moral sense, in that Cipolla's intensification of
the audience's pathological condition eventually results in a
potentially liberating cathartic crisis. That such a crisis *can* be
the beginning of a renewed respect for health and liberty is
apparent not only from the narrator's immediate sense of relief
at Cipolla's death but also from his willingness, as he recounts
his experiences in Italy, to undergo the painful and still far from
complete process of analysing those experiences in order to learn
from them.

Thus, although the story paints a disturbing picture of the
limited and precarious nature of human liberty, it does not do so
in order to encourage fatalistic resignation to the unchangeably
predetermined character of existence. Mann's aim, rather, was
to illuminate the role of historical, social and psychological
conditions in determining the degree of practical, moral freedom
at men's disposal. By drawing such a sombre picture Mann
intended to alert his readers to the gravity and complexity of the

problem: 'Das Böse zu prophezeien ist ja nur meine verzweifelte Art, das Gute zu fordern' (*6*, p.489). A principal value of the story, however, lies in the fact that it does not simply prophesy 'das Böse' but illuminates the quite particular socio-historical conditions under which it can gain power over men. And such knowledge is of the kind 'that maketh free'.

9. The Role of the Narrator

Thomas Mann assigns to the narrator of *Mario und der Zauberer* (who, despite obvious similarities, is not to be identified entirely with the author) a double role in relation to the central problem of freedom. The narrator's function is both to observe the loss of freedom in others and, just as importantly, to bear witness, directly and indirectly, to the erosion of his *own* freedom during the holiday in Torre di Venere. In this respect his narration has something of the character of an exercise in psycho-analysis, for it carries him back to a traumatic past, the memory of which still troubles him, in an effort to understand his experiences and to come to terms with the guilt he feels about the way he behaved. The narrator's record of events exemplifies both the strengths and the limitations of the intellect as a counter-force to the irrational energies embodied in Cipolla: while his vivid memory and analytic powers clarify for the reader the complex connections between Cipolla's power and the prevailing atmosphere in Italian society, the narrator is not able to pin down exactly why he too succumbed to Cipolla to the extent of exposing his whole family to moral danger. By burdening his narrator with unresolved guilt in this way, Thomas Mann cleverly motivated both the narrator's confessional impulse to recount his experiences *and* his partial blindness about his own behaviour. As Sautermeister observes, this device of the imperfect narrator serves a didactic function: 'Dem Leser ist anheimgestellt, die vielerorts unvollendete Aufklärung des Erzählers zu vollenden' (*89*, p.50).

As he reviews his conduct during Cipolla's performance, the narrator repeatedly asks why he did not take the children away from this morally dangerous spectacle. Eventually he concedes that it was probably because he too had become 'infected' by the atmosphere prevailing in the theatre:

...daß wir sie immer noch nicht fortgeschafft hatten, kann ich mir nur mit einer gewissen Ansteckung durch die allgemeine Fahrlässigkeit erklären, von der zu dieser Nachtstunde auch wir ergriffen waren. (p.266)

Clear though this may seem to him in retrospect, however, each of the steps that led to the family's exposure to this moral contagion had seemed harmless at the time. As so often, evil begins in a banal and inconspicuous manner. The 'Ansteckung' in the theatre had been preceded by the infectious but seemingly innocuous enthusiasm of the children to see a real, live magician: 'ein gewisses Zerstreuungsbedürfnis empfanden wir selbst, und die dringende Neugier der Kinder bewährte eine Art von Ansteckungskraft' (p.230).

The decision to go to the show was in turn a consequence of an earlier decision not to leave the resort despite strong feelings of unease. At that point, the narrator recalls, they stayed on in Torre out of a mixture of fascination with the curious, tense atmosphere and a stubborn refusal to be driven away by the first signs of danger and disease:

Wir blieben auch deshalb, weil der Aufenthalt uns merkwürdig geworden war, und weil Merkwürdigkeit ja in sich selbst einen Wert bedeutet, unabhängig von Behagen und Unbehagen. Soll man die Segel streichen und dem Erlebnis ausweichen, sobald es nicht vollkommen danach angetan ist, Heiterkeit und Vertrauen zu erzeugen? Soll man 'abreisen', wenn das Leben sich ein bißchen unheimlich, nicht ganz geheuer oder etwas peinlich und kränkend anläßt? Nein doch, man soll bleiben, soll sich das ansehen und sich dem aussetzen, gerade dabei gibt es vielleicht etwas zu lernen. (p.228)

Clearly, such willingness to witness uncanny or threatening phenomena is necessary if man's understanding of himself, and of the power over him of such things, is to expand.[23] It is even

[23] The ambiguities in the narrator's position are discussed by Bance (57, p.387).

important that the narrator should share with Cipolla certain
attributes, such as an artistic disposition and an accompanying
disdain for the masses, for these provide him with vital, intuitive
insights into the workings of a related mind (as in the case of
Mann's own analysis of the psychology of 'Bruder Hitler'). On
the other hand, as Mann observed in a discussion of Freud's
work, there is a danger that interest in irrational phenomena
may slide imperceptibly into sympathetic identification with
them:

> Ein Interesse gerät sehr leicht in ein Verhältnis der Solid-
> arität und der endgültigen Sympathie mit seinem
> Gegenstande, es gelangt leicht dahin, zu bejahen, was es
> nur zu erkennen ausgegangen war. Ein Interesse ist selbst
> interessant; wo es besteht, ist die Frage, aus welchem
> Grunde und zu welchem Zweck es besteht; es fragt sich
> zum Beispiel, ob ein vorwaltendes Interesse fürs Affektive
> selbst affektiver Natur ist oder von intellektueller Art.
>
> *(10,* Vol.3, p.169)

From the narrator's own account of his experiences in the
course of the holiday it is clear to the reader, if not to the
narrator himself, that his 'Interesse fürs Affektive' is indeed
'selbst affektiver Natur'. As he acknowledges, he was irritated
by the crowds, the noise and the heat, by his treatment at the
hotel and on the beach. But it is also clear that he felt more
aggression than he allowed himself to show — more indeed than
he is even now prepared to admit to. He received in silence the
humiliating sermon from the indignant Italian, biting back the
sarcastic comments he would like to have made, then paying the
fine, again without demur. His one act of protest, which was to
move his family from the Grand Hôtel to the considerably more
modest Pensione Eleonora rather than allow the family to be
moved out to an annexe, is vitiated by the fact that he then takes
the family back to have tea at the hotel periodically ('Dabei
fühlten wir uns mit dem Grand Hôtel nicht einmal überworfen',
p.221) and, what is more, strictly forbids the child with the
offending whooping cough even to clear its throat within earshot

of the princess. The suppression of the cough, banal and even comic in itself, is symptomatic of a deeper stifling of his anger, which is the price the narrator has to pay for the privilege of knowing that he and his family have not been excluded entirely from the distinguished social circles in which they like to move. As Böhme points out (*58*, p.291), the experience of being snubbed and temporarily de-classed leaves the narrator in an ambivalent state of submission to and resentment of the established power-structure in this society.

This sense of injury and the accompanying need to vent his suppressed and only partially acknowledged aggressions then puts the narrator on a similar emotional footing to the rest of the audience at the magician's show. The authoritarian component in his feelings makes him identify, however unwillingly, with the fellow-artist Cipolla's hostile, haughty attitude to the audience, while the submissive, masochistic component in his disposition makes him unable to leave a spectacle which he finds offensive and disturbing — just as he remained attached to the Grand Hôtel despite his professed abhorrence of the 'kriecherischer Korruption' there. Yet it is precisely the fact that the narrator shares with the others the ambiguous mixture of pity and 'grausamer Genugtuung' (p.265) aroused by Cipolla's humiliating abuse of his powers that makes him such a valuable witness. What is more, the inability of even such a relatively intelligent and self-aware witness to answer his own repeated and increasingly anguished questions as to why he did not take himself and his family out of the presence of what he knew to be evil provides the reader with invaluable evidence of the insidious power of subconscious impulse, when exploited by a Cipolla, to create barriers against self-understanding and to undermine the moral will.

10. The Role of Mario

Because *Mario und der Zauberer* is a story with political over-tones some commentators have claimed that Mann's intention was to attack the upper and middle classes in society for collaborating with, or failing to resist, fascism, and to present Mario's shooting of Cipolla as a model of effective working-class resistance to fascism.[24] To what extent is such a reading borne out by the text?

Certainly, the story makes references to social class from the outset. The incident involving the aristocratic Roman lady in the hotel has been taken as a pointer to the connections between the interests of the established, privileged classes and the authoritarian nationalism of the fascists, while the hostility of the crowds of Italian middle-class holiday-makers on the beach has been related to the fact that fascism found considerable support among the lower middle-classes.[25] By contrast, the narrator's children are treated in a friendly way by the local fishermen and by the waiter Mario, which bears out Thomas Mann's own observation after the family holiday in 1926 that 'das eigentliche Volk' had remained relatively unaffected by the 'blähenden Einfluß des Duce' (*87*, p.25).

If the story is examined more closely, however, it is difficult to sustain an analysis based on contrast between the social classes. The description of the road leading to the makeshift theatre, for example, suggestively leads past houses which have associations with *all* different classes, ranging from the aristocratic to the proletarian:

[24] Partisan commentaries of this kind are offered by Diersen (*61*), Matter (*81*), Mayer (*83*) and Richter (*88*). The essays by Schwarz (*90*) and Lunn (*75*) also have a strong, if less partisan, emphasis on class.

[25] See Schwarz (*90*, p.55) and Lunn (*75*, pp.83f.).

Man gelangte dahin, indem man, vorbei am 'Palazzo', einem übrigens verkäuflichen, kastellartigen Gemäuer aus herrschaftlichen Zeiten, die Hauptstraße des Ortes verfolgte, an der auch die Apotheke, der Coiffeur, die gebräuchlichsten Einkaufsläden zu finden waren, und die gleichsam vom Feudalen über das Bürgerliche ins Volkstümliche führte; denn sie lief zwischen ärmlichen Fischerwohnungen aus, vor deren Türen alte Weiber Netze flickten, und hier, schon im Populären, lag die 'Sala' (p.230)

The audience that then assembles in the hall is drawn from all social classes, as it is from a variety of nationalities ('Man hörte Englisch und Deutsch. Man hörte das Französisch, das etwa Rumänen mit Italienern sprechen', p.232).

Cipolla's approach to his audience confirms the impression that it was not Mann's intention to define the appeal of fascism in terms of class or national characteristics.[26] Far from giving any indication that the workers are his 'natural enemies' or any such thing, the hypnotist begins his campaign of manipulation with the ordinary people of Torre: 'Cipolla hütete sich, den vornehmen Teil seines Publikums zu belästigen. Er hielt sich ans Volk' (p.242). The first person to be hypnotized is Giovanotto, and the last is Mario, both of them workers, both of them rivals for the love of the same girl. Between the first and the last demonstration of his powers, however, Cipolla extends the social range from which his victims are drawn to include Signora Angiolieri, who runs the Pensione Eleonora, a 'Colonnello', and the 'Herr aus Rom' who at first puts up strenuous resistance to Cipolla's attempts to break his will. His resistance eventually proves futile, but he holds out longer than either Giovanotto or Mario, who succumb very quickly to Cipolla's power of illusion. Nor are the lower-middle-class crowds at whose hands the narrator experienced the new mood of aggressive nationalism in

[26] Mann stressed the generality of the problem in this observation: 'Aber der Faschismus, von dem der Nationalsozialismus eine eigentümliche Abwandlung ist, ist keine deutsche Spezialität, sondern eine Zeitkrankheit, die überall zu Hause und von der kein Land frei ist' (*10*, Vol.2, p.254).

Italy much in evidence during Cipolla's show because most of them have already returned to their home towns. Far from providing any reassurance, then, that one particular class can remain untouched by a dictatorial will, the story shows the cancer of Cipolla's evil influence eating its way through society indiscriminately. But if an analysis in terms of social class does little to illuminate Mario's role in the story, what does?

In the first instance Mario is suited to become Cipolla's antagonist by virtue of his character and the particular emotional state he happens to be in at the time of their confrontation. By nature he is an unusually reserved person. In fact it is Mario's melancholy 'Zug von Verschlossenheit' (p.271) which excites Cipolla's interest from an early stage in the proceedings, for the magician evidently detects in this reserve (in contrast to the loud-mouthed weakness of Giovanotto) a self-contained strength of character which should provide him with a last, demanding test of his powers. Mario's manner suggests that he wants to preserve from intrusion an inner world of intense feeling, and that he is unwilling to sacrifice personal integrity to vagaries of public mood or to the demands of his work as a waiter. Mario is characterized by his:

> ...träumerische, leicht in Geistesabwesenheit sich verlierende Art, die er in hastigem Übergang durch eine besondere Dienstfertigkeit korrigierte; sie war ernst, höchstens durch die Kinder zum Lächeln zu bringen, nicht mürrisch, aber unschmeichlerisch, ohne gewollte Liebenswürdigkeit' (p.268)

Mario's seriousness and genuineness distinguish him from the bulk of his compatriots whose whole style of life at present is theatrical and has something forced ('gewollt') about it. Whereas many Italians, under the influence of the fascist ethos, have assumed a personality that does not accord with their true feelings, Mario wants to be his own man. What is more, he does so even in the kind of job where a flattering manner is easily developed. Mario's combination of 'Dienstfertigkeit' with a refusal to ingratiate himself with the customers is his way of preserving his qualities of inwardness and independence of spirit in a public, servile occupation, for this allows him to draw a clear line between what he is willing to give his clients and what he must refuse. At the climax of the story Mario acts, not as any waiter would in such circumstances, but as an individual possessed of particular sensitivity and concern for his integrity and whose intense need for privacy is deeply offended by a public trespass across the line of demarcation he habitually insists upon.

At present Mario's inwardness has a particular focus in the person of Silvestra, a girl he loves passionately. Along with that love go feelings of melancholy and jealousy, for he has been rejected by Silvestra in favour of Giovanotto. Although it is not made as plain as it perhaps should be in the story, Mario's disappointment in love explains why he is carrying a revolver on the evening of Cipolla's performance (see 7, p.372). When Cipolla makes the hypnotized Mario believe that Silvestra wants to be kissed by Mario he gives Mario a moment of utterly unexpected happiness, only to follow it with a cruel awakening to sharpened disappointment compounded by the shame of having his private feelings mocked before the gaze of the public. Thus the very strength of feeling which enables Cipolla to delude Mario leads to his death at Mario's hands. In choosing Mario as his last victim, Cipolla unwittingly brings about his own downfall.

This seemingly fortuitous reversal is in fact the fulfilment of a hidden design. Although the hypnotist dies expressing surprise at the outcome, the story makes it clear that subconscious psychological pressures have been at work in Cipolla all along, steering him towards death. As we have seen, Cipolla's life is one founded on power as a substitute for the love he feels he cannot have. In him the frustrated need for love is transformed into hatred and cynicism, but these feelings are accompanied by self-pity ('Sono io il poveretto!') and self-hatred. The will with which he claims to master life has to overcome resistance as much from himself as from others, so that he is increasingly exhausted by his efforts and has to resort to ever more stimulants in order to drive his tired body and spirit on to each new, but fundamentally unsatisfying effort to prove his worth to himself and others. Each time he slumps down after a bout of exertion Cipolla's body is crying out not just for relaxation but for release from the treadmill of a will to power that does not ultimately believe in itself. Cipolla finds that release in death.

Cipolla's fate represents the triumph within his own 'psychic eonomy' of the death instinct, to which Freud gave the mythical name 'Thanatos', over the sexual or life instinct, to which he gave the mythical name 'Eros'.[27] Yet Mario's role is defined not just by Cipolla's individual desire to yield to death, but also by the complementary need of life to assert itself against the forces of death and disease embodied in the magician. At bottom Mario's instinctively and unconsciously performed function is to embody, on behalf of the community, the mythical-psychological resistance of 'Eros' to the destructive force to 'Thanatos'. Deep below the surface of contemporary social and political tensions this is the ancient story of the struggle between winter and spring. As such, Mario's rebellion against Cipolla re-enacts the ritual of 'Vatertötung' analysed by Freud in 'Totem und Tabu' (*36*, Vol.9), an act supposedly made necessary by the sexual monopoly of the older, dominant males in primitive tribes. By flaunting his sexual possessiveness, first by 'seducing' Signora Angiolieri and then by magically appropriating the image of Silvestra, Cipolla invites Mario's violent response. The fact that Mario's action has tragic consequences for himself (he is arrested and will presumably be punished for murder) only strengthens the mythical pattern, for the death of the young hero is a price exacted by tradition for his action on behalf of the tribe.

This role as Cipolla's challenger explains why there is mention of the primitive qualities in Mario's appearance:

Stellen Sie ihn sich vor als einen untersetzt gebauten Jungen von zwanzig Jahren mit kurzgeschorenem Haar, niedriger Stirn und zu schweren Lidern...Das Obergesicht

[27] See Freud's essay 'Jenseits des Lustprinzips' (*36*, Vol.13, pp.3-69).

> mit der eingedrückten Nase, die einen Sattel von Sommer-
> sprossen trug, trat zurück gegen das untere, von den
> dicken Lippen beherrschte, zwischen denen beim Sprechen
> die feuchten Zähne sichtbar wurden, und diese
> Wulstlippen verliehen zusammen mit der Verhülltheit der
> Augen seiner Physiognomie eine primitive Schwermut.
> (p.268)

This description uses elements of the stereotypical negroid face
to suggest that Mario retains certain primitive (and thus
instinctual) qualities in the midst of the modern world. The
description, although not entirely free of racist condescension, is
not negative, but seems intended rather to convey an air of the
'noble savage'; hence the mention of Mario's hands:

> Von Brutalität des Ausdrucks konnte keine Rede sein; dem
> hätte schon die ungewöhnliche Schmalheit und Feinheit
> seiner Hände widersprochen, die selbst unter Südländern
> als nobel auffielen, und von denen man sich gern bedienen
> ließ. (p.268)

This characterization of Mario, which fits into the pattern of
associations linking Cipolla and his audience with the behaviour
of a primitive tribe under the sway of its witch-doctor, reinforces
the pattern of poetic justice as Cipolla falls victim to the very
primitivism he has himself unleashed.

In the later version of the mythical confrontation between
death and life (or dark and light), which casts the life-negating
force in the shape of the devil, Mario plays the role of 'der gute
Junge' to Cipolla's Mephistopheles.[28] As Mann interpreted that
tradition, the defining characteristics of the good young man are
precisely the earnestness and intensity of his love, while the
older, evil figure is defined in terms of the absence or negation
of love: 'Tiefste Lieblosigkeit, funkelnder Haß ist das Wesen der
Gestalt' (*2*, p.676). Because that demonic hatred (whether
understood psychologically or theologically) is at bottom a form

[28] See Mann's essay on Goethe's *Faust* (*2*, p.692).

of self-hatred and self-negation, the devil's ruses ultimately come to naught. Like the 'genasführter Teufel' in the tradition of popular farce, Cipolla is bound to be defeated by a Mario because the sickness and evil he represents are a distortion and a negation of life which will ultimately be rooted out by the healthy life on which such things are parasitic.

To sum up: Mann's conception of the role of Mario is of a piece with his general approach in the story to the problems of the contemporary world. The story contains many allusions to the sphere of politics, but it does not operate as a strict political allegory. The resemblance of Cipolla to Mussolini or Goebbels, or to the intellectual and cultural abetters of fascism, has the effect of reminding the reader of the political background against which the events of the story are set. Mann's approach to the problems of fascism, however, is mainly psychological and ethical rather than directly political. For him fascism was both evil and sick, and as such would inevitably produce the conditions of its own destruction. How this is to be achieved in concrete political terms is not a problem the story addresses, just as it leaves many facets of contemporary political reality (for example, constitutional issues, the role of political parties, the complex relations between politics and economics) out of account. Far from representing a concrete political programme, Mario's unreflecting, explosive assault on his tormentor raises the question as to *how* to bring about the unity of 'Geist' and 'Tat' demanded so blithely by Mann's brother Heinrich.[29] The most Mann can offer at the end of his story is the hope that the positive force of love will prove itself stronger than that of death, even if it has to do so by killing in the name of life. Better still would be to ensure that the political and social conditions are not allowed to arise which eventually make necessary such costly acts of liberation.

[29] As Schwarz has pointed out, 'Torre di Venere' is also to be found in Heinrich Mann's novel *Die kleine Stadt*, of which *Mario und der Zauberer* may be a 'Kontrafaktur' (*90*, p.49).

11. Aspects of Narration

The Illusion of Reality

Eduard Korrodi, one of the earliest reviewers of *Mario und der Zauberer*, characterized the active role of Mann's imagination in reworking the stuff of experience in this story very aptly when he wrote: 'Nur ein rechtmäßiger Zauberer der Sprache konnte den andern, die rationale Welt beklemmenden Hexer in einem so skurrilen, wirklich-unwirklichen Spiel beschwören und vernichten' (in *87*, p.32). Nevertheless, Thomas Mann took considerable trouble to persuade the reader of the reality of the fictional town of Torre di Venere so as to suggest to the reader that the events of the story are closely bound up with the real world of contemporary Italy. The impression that the story is drawn directly from life is created, for example, not only by references to such familiar things as the 'Duce' or 'Fiat-Wagen' or the 'Corriere della Sera'[30], but also to the odd hairstyle that has recently become fashionable with the country's pro-fascist youth, this being the kind of detail which gives the story the character of a report from a sharp-eyed and well-informed observer. This effect of authenticity is also produced by the withholding of a factual detail like the full name of the Roman aristocrat ('ein Principe X', p.219), since this suggests that there are real people involved whose reputation needs to be protected by a cloak of anonymity.

The many snatches of Italian cited in the story are a further potent source of the effect of realism. Again, the persuasiveness derives not only from such relatively familiar or recognizable linguistic items as 'Cavaliere' or 'ragazzo mio' or 'poveretto', or

[30] This once liberal newspaper quickly became 'fascisticized' in the 1920s.

from common names like Mario or Giovanotto, but also from
particular details or subtleties either in what is quoted or in the
way it is quoted. When the narrator tries to relax on the beach,
for example, his pleasure is marred not just by the strident voices
of anxious Italian mothers but also by irritating dialectal
impurities, such as one woman's pronunciation of the word
'rispondi': 'Wobei das sp populärerweise nach deutscher Art wie
sch gesprochen wurde — ein Ärgernis für sich, wenn sowieso
üble Laune herrscht' (p.223). As I. Jonas has pointed out (*46*,
p.64), sometimes the narrator's borrowings from the Italian are
only hinted at by some oddity in the German, as when he has
Cipolla say 'siehe ein bißchen' or 'sage ein bißchen', phrases
which, as literal translations of the Italian idioms 'vede un po' or
'dime un po', give the impression that the narrator is recording
faithfully what he has actually heard. This impression is further
reinforced when the narrator bears out one spectator's praise for
Cipolla's mastery of his own tongue ('Parla benissimo'), by
quoting several expamples of more or less subtle word-play:
'linguista di belle speranze' (p.238), 'torregiano di Venere'
(p.244), 'sulla linguaccia' (p.244) or 'salvietta' (p.270).

If references to unfamiliar facts or words are one means of
creating an impression of authenticity, appeals to 'unserer
Vertrautheit mit den Dingen' (*51*, p.476) are no less important
for the achievement of the realist illusion. These appeals can be
explicit, as in such phrases as 'Wie es aber mit solchen Plätzen zu
gehen pflegt' (p.216), or when the narrator dispenses with an
exhaustive account of all Cipolla's experiments: 'Auch langweile
ich Sie nicht mit der Schilderung dieser Versuche; jeder kennt
sie, jeder hat einmal daran teilgenommen' (p.252). Often there is
no need for any explicit appeal to the reader's familiarity, for
'jeder' (of a certain generation, that is) would be bound to
recognize the poster advertising Cipolla's show, for example, as
typical of its kind:

...ein fahrender Virtuose, ein Unterhaltungskünstler,
Forzatore, Illusionista und Prestidigitatore (so bezeich-
nete er sich), welcher dem hochansehnlichen Publikum
von Torre di Venere mit einigen außerordentlichen

Phänomenen geheimnisvoller und verblüffender Art
aufzuwarten beabsichtigte. (p.229)

So confident is Mann of the reader's familiarity with what he
describes that he can reduce a description to the barest outline:
the single word 'Gehrockmanager' characterizes the figure with
striking economy.

Mann's gift for visual description contributes in various ways
to the effect of realism. Again, this can take the form of an
appeal to the familiar, as in this carefully structured verbal
snapshot of the coastline around Torre: 'Da der Strand,
begleitet von Piniengehölz, auf das aus geringer Entfernung die
Berge herniederblicken, diese ganze Küste entlang seine
wohnlich-feinsandige Geräumigkeit behält...'(p.215). The
vignettes of the 'Fischerwohnungen...vor deren Türen alte
Weiber Netze flickten' (p.230) or of the netsmen at work in the
reddish light of evening ('bloßbeinige...stemmend und ziehend,
unter gedehnten Rufen', p.231), which also come into this
category, may owe the effect of recognition as much to the
reader's familiarity with paintings as to actual experience of the
things described. Yet Mann's 'pen-drawings' do not rely on
recognition alone for the effect of realism. As with his rendering
of details of speech, Mann repeatedly focusses on some visual
oddity that seems 'real' to the reader because of the sharpness
and immediacy with which the description etches itself in the
imagination. A good example of this technique is the moment
when Mario, awakened from his trance, throws himself into a
curious, backward-leaning position: 'Er stand und starrte,
hintübergebogenen Leibes, drückte die Hände an seine
mißbrauchten Lippen, eine über der anderen, schlug sich dann
mit den Knöcheln beider mehrmals gegen die Schläfen...'(p.274).

The verisimilitude of the story has as much to do with the
manner of its telling as with what is described or narrated. In
particular, the illusion that it is an account of real events is
supported by the continuing and quite apparent effect on the
narrator of his experiences in Torre di Venere. From the very
first sentence ('Die Erinnerung an Torre di Venere ist atmosphärisch unangenehm', p.215), Thomas Mann makes the reader

aware that the events of the story are being recounted from the
perspective of someone who is still wrestling with what his
memories of the holiday imply both for his view of life generally
and, more specifically, for his own moral self-perception. This
unifying perspective motivates the coherence of the story, for
the reader is aware of the selective operation of the narrator's
memory as it focuses on events lodged there by his mixed
feelings of irritation, fascination and guilt. The more we learn of
what happened to the family in Torre the better we understand
the narrator's complex attitude, and the more we understand his
feelings the more real seem the experiences that gave rise to
them. A clear example of the way the strength of the narrator's
feelings lends both immediacy and credibility to what he is
describing occurs during Cipolla's 'duel' with the gentleman
from Rome:

> 'Auch wenn Sie nicht wollen!' antwortete Cipolla in einem
> Ton, der mir unvergeßlich ist. Ich habe dies fürchterliche
> 'Anche se non vuole!' noch immer im Ohr. (p.264)

In circumstances where an account is being given from a freely
acknowledged personal point of view ('ich war gereizt, ich wollte
es vielleicht empfinden' — p.222 — admits the narrator at one
stage), the style of presentation is bound to deviate from
standards of strict, dispassionate objectivity if the illusion of
realism is to be sustained. Thus the narrator's account is made
more rather than less plausible when he indulges from time to
time in outright sarcasm ('das antikische Heldenjammergeschrei', 'jener Gestrenge im steifen Hut').[31] A related effect is
produced by the narrator's imperfections as a chronicler, such as
his inability to remember certain things as clearly as he would
like, or his apology for recounting things out of their proper
order:

> Ich habe vorgegriffen und die Reihenfolge ganz beiseite
> geworfen. Mein Kopf ist noch heute voll von Erinnerungen

[31] See the essay by Seiler (*51*, p.461).

an des Cavaliere Duldertaten, nur weiß ich nicht mehr
Ordnung darin zu halten, und es kommt auf sie auch nicht
an. (p.260)

The realism of the story is sustained even when Mann
introduces the extraordinary in the shape of Cipolla and his
uncanny powers. The climatic conditions which in retrospect can
be seen to presage his arrival, the mercilessly burning sun
succeeded by oppressive 'Sciroccoschwüle' (p.229), seem at first
sight to be entirely natural and typical of the region. As the
family walk to the *municipio* to see Cipolla's show, the
atmosphere is close and there are occasional flashes of lightning,
but the hints of something ominous in the air are held in check
by the fact that the family responds to the weather in a banal,
matter-of-fact manner by simply putting up their umbrellas: 'Es
war schwül wie seit Tagen, es wetterleuchtete manchmal und
regnete etwas. Wir gingen unter Schirmen. Es war eine
Viertelstunde Weges' (p.230). Similarly, Thomas Mann lends
plausibility to a figure whose demonic aspect becomes ever
more apparent by equipping Cipolla with the typically
extravagant clothes and manner of a fairground showman.
Realism is preserved too by the simple device of explicitly
remarking on the odd and even fantastic impression prov-
oked by his appearance ('der Eindruck reklamehafter und
phantastischer Narretei', pp.233f.) or certain of his more
extreme experiments: 'Der Anblick...war unglaubwürdig und
scheußlich' (p.260).

The various forms of realism in *Mario und der Zauberer* serve
at least three principal functions. The many references to
verifiable facts have the effect of inviting the reader to take
seriously the story's engagement with contemporary reality,
particularly in its social-political aspect. The careful observation
and detailed documentation of behaviour and atmosphere aim
to make plausible the appearance of even as demonic a figure
as Cipolla and the extraordinary powers he is able to exercise in
this milieu. The realism of immediacy, whether in the form of
sharply seen or heard details or in the emotional responses of the
narrator and his family, complements the realism of apparent

facticity by confronting the reader very directly with the
experiences the narrator is still trying to come to terms with, so
that he too is made to feel personally challenged by them. The
irony of the story is given a far sharper edge if the reader
experiences it from the position of at least partial identification
with the narrator.

Genre

Having established that *Mario und der Zauberer* aims at the
effect of realism in a variety of ways, it also has to be pointed
out that the realism of the story is kept within certain well-
defined limits. The narrator's colloquialisms, exclamations or
questions ('Mögen Sie das? Mögen Sie es wochenlang?', p.222)
directed to an assumed interlocutor ('Sie haben recht', p.222),
for example, contrast with the more elevated, complex,
distinctly literary style in which much of the story is told. In a
work of rigorous naturalism such stylistic variability would have
to be criticized as inconsistent and hence unrealistic. To criticize
Mario und der Zauberer in these terms, however, would be to
fail to recognize that Thomas Mann was working here within the
conventions of a particular genre, the *Novelle*.

While it is now generally agreed that no single definition will
cover the many different stories regarded as *Novellen* by their
authors or readers, there does exist a loose, historically evolving
set of characteristics which link such stories in a kind of family
resemblance. The mixture of colloquial and written styles in
Mario und der Zauberer, for example, picks up a strand in the
tradition of *Novelle*-narration that reaches back through
Goethe's *Unterhaltungen deutscher Ausgewanderten* to
Boccaccio's *Decamerone*, namely the fictional convention that
the narrator of the *Novelle* is one of a group of people, often
travellers, who tell stories to one another for their mutual
entertainment, solace or instruction, or, as Goethe put it,
'lehrreich, nützlich und besonders gesellig zu sein'.[32] That

[32] Quoted in the appendix in Paulin (*48*, p.129).

original circle of listeners to which the story is addressed can, in later works, be reduced to just one listener (as in the framework narrative in Theodor Storm's *Der Schimmelreiter*), or it may merely be hinted at in the *manner* of narration, as Friedrich Schlegel implied when he defined the *Novelle* as 'eine noch unbekannte Geschichte, so erzählt, wie man sie in Gesellschaft erzählen würde' (in *48*, p.133). The 'willing suspension of disbelief' practised by any reader of fiction involves accepting that this convention of the spoken narrative is being deployed in *Mario und der Zauberer*.[33]

To take another aspect of the story, the peripeteia or reversal that occurs when Mario avenges his humiliation by shooting Cipolla represents the kind of inner and outer *Wendepunkt* which Ludwig Tieck considered particularly characteristic of the *Novelle*. As the story rises through degrees of intensity to that climax, it exhibits that affinity with the drama stressed by a later master of the genre, Theodor Storm. The demonic aura surrounding Cipolla picks up yet another strand in the tradition, namely the notion that the *Novelle* is a genre that appeals particularly to the 'entschiedene Neigung unserer Natur, das Wunderbare zu glauben' (Goethe, in *48*, p.131). On the other hand, the great care taken by Thomas Mann to root the extraordinary events of the story firmly in the social and psychological conditions of contemporary reality satisfies the complementary demand made by Goethe that the *Novelle* should remain plausible even when recounting something quite out of the ordinary ('eine unerhörte, *sich ereignete* Begebenheit' [my italic] — quoted in *48*, p.93). With its subtle handling of the complex, ambiguous relations between 'the real' and 'the fantastic', between the particular events that supposedly took place in Torre di Venere and the wider spheres of social and political life, between the eccentric individual Cipolla and the mass of ordinary people in his audience, *Mario und der*

[33] Mann was irritated by Julius Bab's criticism of the 'stiff' style of the story, insisting 'Die Geschichte ist ja *gesprochen*, ganz natürlich' (*7*, p.367). When Mann read the story in public before it appeared in print the reporter of the *Neue Berliner 12 Uhr Zeitung* commented: 'Er liest lebhaft, mit kleinen, unterstreichenden, anfeuernden Gesten, sichtlich selbst interessiert an dem Objekt seiner Vorlesung'.

Zauberer stands firmly in a well-established tradition of narrative that had produced some of the most interesting short fiction in Germany during the previous century and a half.[34]

The purpose of this brief outline of the characteristics which identify *Mario und der Zauberer* as an example of its genre is not just to put the story into some convenient literary-historical pigeon-hole. My point is rather that the reader, for all the realism of the story, retains throughout a more or less clear awareness of the artificial, fictional nature of the account he is reading. This is important for Thomas Mann's purposes, in that the kind of illusion he creates in the story is different in kind and intention from that of a Cipolla. Whereas the evil in Cipolla's treatment of his audience is tied up with the completeness and compulsiveness of the illusion, or rather delusion, he awakens in them by exploiting their hidden desires, Thomas Mann's self-consciously fictional form of illusion permits the reader to preserve a certain aesthetic distance from the characters and events conjured up in his mind's eye by the story-teller. This aesthetic freedom is in turn the condition of the reader's ability to perceive the wider implications of the story. Only if the sense of immediacy and reality is balanced by a degree of aesthetic distance is the reader able to perceive the symbolic dimensions of figures, places, events, in other words to recognize the story as what Cervantes called an 'exemplary tale' ('novela ejemplar'), and hence engage with the general moral and political questions at issue. The following sections of this analysis will therefore be concerned with the specific ways in which Thomas Mann's conscious artistic arrangement and structuring of his material contributed to his aims.

---

[34] For a discussion of the ambiguities and tensions explored by the genre, see Swales (*52, passim*).

Artistic Integration

Like many other examples of the genre, *Mario und der Zauberer* is a *Novelle* that seeks not merely to entertain ('delectare') but also to be of moral and intellectual value ('prodesse').[35] In works of this kind the artistic difficulty lies in the integration of these two aspects so that the reader is not disturbed by any suspicion that he is being preached at or being offered a sugared pill. Thomas Mann's awareness of the problem rises to the surface of the story in a passing remark to the listener or reader: 'Ich halte Ihnen keinen Vortrag, aber...' (p.225). How then does Mann achieve the aim of integrating 'prodesse' and 'delectare' in a satisfying artistic whole?

The first challenge facing any story-teller is simply how to hold the reader's attention. The commonest means to this end is the plot, a forward driving action, usually generated by conflict, that keeps the reader asking 'what next?' In *Mario und der Zauberer* a plot of sorts begins to unfold about a quarter of the way into the story when the narrator and his family go to the *municipio* to see Cipolla's show. The principal actors in this plot are Cipolla, of course, and his audience, and the events of the evening are held together not only by the fact that they all have to do with Cipolla's experiments, but also by an emotional tension between the magician and his audience that already begins to make itself felt during the unusually long delay before the beginning of the performance. Here the reader is carried forward by the desire to know what form the next demonstration of Cipolla's powers will take, and whether the feelings of resentment and rebellion in his audience will eventually prove stronger than the hypnotist's ability to make them submit to his will. The impetus linking episode to episode is further sustained by the device of intensification, as Cipolla's experiments intrude ever more intolerably into the private feelings of his subjects, while the resistance to his arrogance rises from Giovanotto's

---

[35] Stefan Großmann, an early reviewer of the story, commented: 'Man sieht, *Mario und der Zauberer* ist eine sehr spannende Sommernovelle, von jungen Damen auf dem Strande zu lesen. Aber auch Ministerpräsidenten sollten sie in den Ferienkoffer packen' (quoted in *87*, p.45).

easily disposed of challenges through the greater stubbornness of the 'Colonnello' and the 'Herr aus Rom' to Mario's seemingly easy compliance followed by his sudden, violent revenge. The drama of these rising tensions is underlined by the gradual approximation of 'Erzählzeit' (narrative time) and 'erzählte Zeit' (narrated time) towards the end, and by Mann's increasing use of the dramatic medium of dialogue as the climactic moment approaches.[36]

But what of the first part of the story? How is the reader's interest held in that long preamble before the appearance of Cipolla in town? Here Mann uses another device to create suspense, by first pointing forward to the eventual collision ('Choc') with Cipolla in the opening paragraph, but then allowing the narrator to digress into a series of reminiscences which lack any linking thread of action, so that the reader is left for a good number of pages to wonder *when* the action proper will begin rather than 'what next?'. The parallel with the delaying tactics later used by Cipolla is striking, and it seems likely that Mann (like Cipolla) used this device of delay to produce a certain impatience and irritation in the reader, thereby attuning him to the mood prevailing in Torre before Cipolla's appearance there. However, Mann also uses this delay to integrate the preamble with the main body of the story in other, less emotive ways. In this section he carefully lays the psychological foundations on which Cipolla's relationship with his audience will rest, and, through the questions and generalizations of the narrator, encourages a reflective, analytic response in the reader to the incidents described. This reflective approach is then carried over into the narrator's account of Cipolla's show. As a result, the conventional plot of events is subsumed in an intellectual plot, the simple question 'what next?' being extended to include the larger and more absorbing questions as to how and why the fascinating and disturbing events of the story could come about.

Although Mann's principal means of alerting the reader to the symbolic implications of events is explicit reflection and

36 See Böhme, *58*, p.27.

commentary on the part of the narrator, he avoids the danger of obtrusive didacticism by the clever way he embeds these reflections in the narrative. They contribute, for example, to the rhythm of the story by providing a welcome periodic respite from the descriptions of conflict, thus creating little plateaux on the steadily rising curve of tension. The reflections during Cipolla's evening are made to seem particularly natural by the fact that they coincide with the pauses interspersed by Cipolla himself. The narrator's observations are also well motivated, both during the evening (when they are mostly prompted by his concern for the children as the hour gets later), and during the act of narration as he is puzzled, moved and irritated by his memories of the things he has experienced. Consequently, far from being felt as intrusive, the narrator's comments are welcomed by the reader for the contribution they make to his own intellectual mastery of the disturbing experiences recorded in the story.

Leitmotif and Symbol

As is almost invariably the case in Thomas Mann's fiction the techniques of leitmotif and symbolism are his most powerful means of unifying *Mario und der Zauberer* and of making the story intellectually transparent. Sometimes the motifs themselves are abstract (e.g. 'Freiheit' and 'Notwendigkeit'), sometimes symbolic (e.g. clothing or parts of the body), and in many cases they take the form of pairs of thematic adjectives (e.g. 'gesund' and 'krank').[37] By subtly interweaving these motifs into numerous interlocking patterns of antithesis, parallelism and variation Mann achieves a fine balance between intellectual transparency and naturalness of presentation.

Mann begins to spin the threads of motifs from the moment the story begins. The phrase 'atmosphärisch unangenehm' (p.215) in the first sentence, for example, is linked by its metaphorical sense to the phrase 'das...Bösartige der Stimmung'

[37] For a discussion of such 'thematische Adjektivierung' see Weiß (*96*, pp.10f.).

in sentence two, but the meteorological associations of 'Atmosphäre' (in the phrases 'lagen von Anfang an in der Luft' and 'sich...bedrohlich zusammenzudrängen schien', p.215) also point forward to the actual influence of the weather on the behaviour of people in Torre di Venere. This to-and-fro between the weather as something natural and the prevailing emotional and intellectual climate in the town is sustained throughout the story, but the motifs are also extended and elaborated, by means of allusion, to encompass political and mythical meanings. Thus the connotations of a brewing storm in the words 'sich bedrohlich zusammendrängen' are picked up in the change to sultry, thundery weather that immediately precedes the arrival of Cipolla:

> Der Himmel bedeckte sich, nicht daß es frischer geworden wäre, aber die offene Glut, die achtzehn Tage seit unserer Ankunft (und vorher wohl lange schon) geherrscht hatte, wich einer stickigen Sciroccoschwüle, und ein schwächlicher Regen netzte von Zeit zu Zeit den samtenen Schauplatz unserer Vormittage. (p.229)

These are the first signs of the storm which arrives with rain and lightning on the evening of Cipolla's performance.

The language in which Cipolla's performance is announced also has meteorological overtones: 'Zu diesem Zeitpunkt also zeigte Cipolla sich an' (p.229) — 'sich anzeigen' being a phrase that can apply to an incipient change in the weather. Underpinning these verbal links in turn is a traditional superstitious association of sudden changes in the weather (usually for the worse) with the appearance of evil, demonic forces; hence the first flickers of lightning ('es wetterleuchtete manchmal', p.230) on the actual night of the performance. As Walter Weiß has pointed out (*96*, p.84), the 'flach schmetternde Detonationen' (p.274) from Mario's pistol symbolize on the level of human action the outbreak of the long awaited thunder, the sense of relief produced by this 'befreiendes Ende' being the emotional equivalent of the sudden release of tension in a thunderstorm.

Yet the weather has also been unpleasant in a different way

long before Cipolla appears. For weeks the holidaymakers in Torre have sweltered under the excessive, unrelieved heat of the sun:

> Die Hitze war unmäßig, soll ich das anführen? Sie war afrikanisch: die Schreckensherrschaft der Sonne...von einer Unerbittlichkeit, die die wenigen Schritte vom Strande zum Mittagstisch selbst im bloßen Pyjama, zu einem im voraus beseufzten Unternehmen machte. (p.222)

Here the sun forms part of a tight knot of motif-threads that is very typical of Mann's method of composition. Firstly, the personification of the sun as a tyrannical ruler ('Schreckens-herrschaft', 'Unerbittlichkeit', 'übermütig waltete') fore-shadows Cipolla's tyranny over his audience, Cipolla being described repeatedly as 'schrecklich' and in the vocabulary of rule: 'unser Gebieter' (p.256), 'herrschte unumschränkt' (p.266), 'Der Herr des Abends' (p.267), 'eines so im Erfolg thronenden Mannes' (p.267). Conversely, the holidaymakers who submit both to the tyranny of the sun and to the prevailing mood of irritability ('ein Ärgernis für sich, wenn sowieso üble Laune *herrscht*' [my italic], p.223) exhibit a passivity that Cipolla knows how to exploit so skilfully. The torpor of the people is matched by that of the waves, slow and slack in the period before the storm, and mirrored in the spineless jellyfish washing to and fro among them: 'das schlaffe, entfärbte Meer, in dessen Flachheit träge Quallen trieben' (p.229). The adjectives 'träge' and 'schlaff', which belong to the same motif-chain as 'lässig', are typical of Mann's technique of relating the physical aspects of men's lives to their psychological and moral states. In the sudden change from raging heat to listlessness, however, there is also a strong suggestion that the whole natural world is succumbing to a feverish disease, a suggestion which stresses the larger-than-life, i.e. mythical, dimensions of Mario's clash with the demonic Cipolla.

The characterization of the sun as 'afrikanisch' forms part of another network of associations which include Giovanotto's 'fascist' haircut: 'Er trug sein schwarzes, starres Kraushaar hoch und wild, die Modefrisur des erweckten Vaterlandes, die ihn etwas entstellte und afrikanisch anmutete' (p.236). Implied in this area of imagery are notions of the primitive and the instinctual, which are then developed in Mario's negroid physiognomy with its 'primitiver Schwermut' and in the 'tribal dance' presided over by the magician Cipolla. This dance is explicitly a 'Step', one of the so-called 'negro dances' which arrived in Europe in the 1920s along with jazz. The fact that such dances were officially disapproved of in fascist Italy[38] is one of the details which make Cipolla's role complementary to rather than simply a mirror of Mussolini's, in that he exposes the emotions repressed by the ethos of discipline and asceticism. A further anticipatory link with the climax of Cipolla's evening is implicit in the description of the heat of the sun as 'unmäßig', for Cipolla's 'dionysian' power has the effect of making the audience lose all sense of measure ('Maß') as they swing from one extreme of repressive, puritanical control to the opposite extreme of 'trunkener Auflösung' during the dance.

In *Mario und der Zauberer* the sun ('die Sonne Homers', p.222) exercises the fearsome power which the ancient Greeks attributed to the sun-god Apollo, bringer of drought, disease and pestilence.[39] In this story, as in the myths of the Greeks, the power of the sun causes not joy but exhaustion, not health but the 'ekelerregende Sonnenbrandwunde' (p.223) exhibited by the morally repulsive Fuggiero. Here the sun is not associated, as it was in the Enlightenment, with the light of reason, but with irrational, heated anger such as that of the Italian on the beach ('Dem erhitzten Menschen', p.226). This emphasis on the heat rather than the light of the sun gives rise to a series of motifs linking it with the baleful influence of Cipolla. The magician's eyes, focus of his hypnotic power, are described as 'zugleich welk und brennend' (p.245) during hypnosis, in a paradoxical mixture of lassitude and intensity which suggests that at such moments he becomes the channel of some greater force. The fiery sun was also the eye of Apollo (whose other symbols, the

[38] See Mack Smith, *29*, p.161.

[39] Nietzsche plays down these aspects of Apollo in *Die Geburt der Tragödie*.

hawk and the goat, are hinted at in Cipolla's claw-handed whip and his satyr-like walk, while Apollo's feared 'Spitzpfeiler' find their counterpart in Cipolla's sharp words, looks, fingers and teeth). As we have seen, Cipolla is further associated with fire by virtue of the streams of smoke he exhales during each pause in his performance. By interweaving in this way Christian and pagan strands in the symbolism of sun and fire, Thomas Mann relates the contemporary recrudescence of primitive emotions to an excess in nature on the one hand and to an accompanying disturbance of the moral order on the other, both of which will eventually be righted by the inherent balance in life.[40]

If the motifs derived from the weather illustrate well Mann's use of parallelism and variation as techniques of integration, his presentation of individual appearance or behaviour provides good examples of the complementary technique of antithesis. Cipolla's appearance, for instance, dominated as it is by the qualities of ugliness, falsity, sharpness and blackness, is a symbolic complex with strong demonic connotations. Mario's role as his principal antagonist is similarly underscored by many details of his appearance which are antithetical to that of Cipolla. Mario's white waiter's uniform, for example, seems to suit him particularly well: 'Die weiße Jacke, in der er servierte, kleidete ihn besser als der verschossene Complet aus dünnem, gestreiftem Stoff, in dem er jetzt da hinaufstieg' (pp.268f.). Whereas Cipolla's eyes are not only 'streng' (p.234) but, as befits a devil who bores his way into the souls of men, 'scharf' and 'stechend' (p.233), Mario's eyes have a dreamy, heavy-lidded, veiled quality ('mit...zu schweren Lidern', 'mit der Verhülltheit der Augen', p.268) which signals his tendency to withdraw into his own, intensely private world. The sharpness of Cipolla's eyes is matched by that of his teeth ('zwischen seinen schadhaft abgenutzten, spitzigen Zähnen', p.235) and claw-like hands ('mit spitzen Fingern', p.234, 'mit allen seinen zehn langen und gelben Fingern', p.261), whereas Mario has beautiful, healthy teeth ('ein Lachen sehr gesunder Zähne', p.231) and hands ('die ungewöhnliche Schmalheit und Feinheit

[40] Both McIntyre (*77*, p.216) and Dierks (*60*, p.179) stress this notion of balance.

seiner Hände', p.268). While Cipolla's hair is 'sehr häßlich' in the way it attempts to disguise his true age ('nur eine schmale, schwarz gewichste Scheitelfrisur lief, wie angeklebt, vom Wirbel nach vorn, während das Schläfenhaar, ebenfalls geschwärzt, seitlich zu den Augenwinkeln hingestrichen war', p.240), Mario's short-cropped hair is as unpretentious as his character. Just as Cipolla's ugliness is unmistakably the outward sign of his defective character (his 'Gehässigkeit'), so Mario's quietly pleasing appearance expresses the inherent nobility of his nature.

Complexity and Irony

Important as parallelism and antithesis were to Thomas Mann as devices for structuring his fiction, his understanding of reality could not be adequately expressed just in terms of similarity and contrast, no matter how subtly shaded. Just as Mann was later to insist that the problem of Germany's surrender to National Socialism could never be grasped properly by anyone who thought in terms of a straightforward opposition between a 'good' Germany on the one hand and a 'bad' Germany on the other (see *10*, Vol.2, p.297), so *Mario und der Zauberer* resists too simple a view of the problems it tackles by presenting the reader with paradoxes, conflicts of value, and unsettling connections between seeming opposites.

During his evening of experiments Cipolla makes the body of one of his subjects go stiff as a board, so stiff in fact that he can squat ('hocken') on it like some incubus or devil taking possession of its victim. By contrast, when Cipolla makes this selfsame young man lead the audience into a hypnotic dance later in the evening, the descriptions repeatedly use words signifying 'loosening' or 'looseness': 'eine trunkene Auflösung der kritischen Widerstände' (p.263), 'auf einmal lösten sich alle seine Gelenke' (p.265), 'die Gelöstheit des Saales' (p.266). These contrasting effects of rigidity and looseness acquire their symbolic meaning through their place in the story's network of symbolism. The 'brettstarre Körper' of the young hypnotic subject is linked by association to the earlier scene in which the irate Italian delivers a pompously worded sermon on the beach while wearing an incongruous 'steifen Hut' (p.227), an apt symbol of his moral rigidity. However, as was apparent to the narrator at the time, the man's moralizing tirade was actually the vehicle for passions that were not truly moral in character. In this 'Philippika...in der alles Pathos des sinnenfreudigen Südens sich in den Dienst spröder Zucht und Sitte gestellt findet' (p.226), the man's repressed emotional energies merely ape the forms of moral outrage in order to find a socially sanctioned outlet. Paradoxically then the little Italian's tirade on the virtue of self-*discipline* was itself a perverse form of self-*indulgence*, a disguised release of unacknowledged, bottled-up passions. Precisely this psychological unity of opposites is mirrored in Cipolla's trick of making one and the same individual 'stocksteif' at one moment and turning him into a loose-limbed dancer the next: 'in einer Art von wohlgefälliger Ekstase mit geschlossenen Augen und wiegendem Kopf seine dürftigen Glieder nach allen Seiten zu schleudern' (p.264). In this way Mann not only shows that the excessive moral rigidity of the fascist mentality is likely to collapse into the 'opposite' extreme of a moral and emotional licence which it both nourishes and feeds on, he also shows both extremes to be interchangeable forms of the same fundamental loss of human autonomy and dignity.

Irony is a particular form of the unity of opposites. Its simplest form is the use of words to signify the opposite of what they normally denote, as when the narrator tries to excuse the offence unwittingly committed by his little daughter by pointing out 'das zarte Alter, die leibliche Unbeträchtlichkeit der jungen *Delinquentin*' [my italic] (p.227). A more complicated form of irony (often referred to as 'dramatic' irony) occurs when an action leads to the opposite of the intended effect, as when Oedipus, precisely by attempting to avoid the terrible things prophesied by the oracle, brings these very things about. In *Mario und der Zauberer* the smaller, simpler forms of irony are often building blocks in larger, more complex ironic patterns.

Cipolla habitually uses verbal irony in the form of sarcasm as

a means of asserting or reasserting his superiority in a situation
where he feels it to be threatened or undermined. Thus he tries to
cope with his own jealousy towards the robust and handsome
Giovanotto by praising the younger man in high-flown terms
that are clearly intended to ridicule him while at the same time
exhibiting the magician's superior wit: 'ich habe es jetzt mit
diesem Ehrenmann zu tun, con questo torregiano di Venere,
diesem Türmer der Venus, der sich zweifellos süßer
Danksagungen versieht für seine Wachsamkeit' (p.244).
Through the workings of dramatic irony, however, each step
Cipolla takes to increase his personal power in compensation for
the love his life lacks, leads ultimately to his being killed by
Mario for mocking Mario's love.

Although the narrator derives evident satisfaction from
having observed this ironic outcome, he in his turn becomes the
object of narrative irony. Retrospectively the narrator too 'tries
to impose his command by irony' (Bance, 57, p.391), as in his
account of the family's brief stay in the Grand Hôtel. From his
own evidence it is clear that the Roman noblewoman who made
a fuss about the child's whooping cough was the true cause of
the family's embarrassment. Yet the narrator tries to direct his
irritation as far as possible onto the hotel manager who has the
unenviable task of appeasing this difficult but influential client;
hence his self-correction as soon as he begins to describe the
conflict: 'Aber mit gewissen Verandaklienten, *oder richtiger
wohl nur* mit der Hotelleitung, die vor ihnen liebedienerte, ergab
sich sogleich einer dieser Konflikte...' [my italic], (pp.218f.).
The equivocating 'wohl' here gives the game away, just as it does
when he tries to put the blame for his humiliating treatment on
the manager rather than on the princess who is so clearly to
blame:

Es ist *unwahrscheinlich*, daß die wortbrüchige Hart-
näckigkeit, auf die wir stießen, diejenige der Fürstin war.
Der servile Gastwirt hatte *wohl* nicht einmal gewagt, ihr
von dem Votum des Doktors Mitteilung zu machen [my
italic] (p.220)

While concentrating fierce sarcasm on the 'Byzantinismus' of the 'servile Gastwirt', the narrator leans over backwards to make allowances for the princess's superstitious ignorance:

> Das Wesen dieser Krankheit ist wenig geklärt, dem Aberglauben hier mancher Spielraum gelassen, und so haben wir es unserer eleganten Nachbarin nie verargt, daß sie der weitverbreiteten Meinung anhing, der Keuchhusten sei akustisch ansteckend. (p.219)

In fact, however, he *is* angry with her, but tries to play down his irritation by using a relatively mild, humorous form of irony: 'Im weiblichen Vollgefühl ihres Ansehens wurde sie vorstellig bei der Direktion' (p.219). A later, rather too waspish thumbnail sketch of the lady's appearance in the hotel garden betrays a keener resentment than his humorously understanding attitude would have us believe:

> ...nicht ohne der Fürstin ansichtig zu werden, welche, die Lippen korallenrot aufgehöht, mit zierlich festen Schritten erschien, um sich nach ihren von einer Engländerin betreuten Lieblingen umzusehen (p.222)

Reading between the lines, the narrator's ambiguities insinuate that this 'leidenschaftliche Mutter' (p.219) is overweight ('*Voll*gefühl', 'mit zierlich *festen* Schritten' [my italic]), rather tartish in appearance ('Lippen korallenrot aufgehöht'), and less caring about her 'darlings' than her occasional visits to them are meant to convey.

Therefore, despite the narrator's attempts to control the reader's, and his own, view of the situation by the use of irony, the contradictions and uncertainties in his account make his own behaviour seem suspect. It is not hard to detect the class prejudice underlying his account, the ingrained habit of 'kicking the servants' when masters or mistresses are annoyed with one another. The 'bekannte Gehrockmanager' is simply the first person to take the brunt of the narrator's annoyance at his exclusion from an elite to which he still likes to think he belongs. In treating him like this, the narrator is, ironically, guilty of the

very same 'Mißbrauch der Macht' (even if only in words) which
he complains of in others.

Inconsistencies of this kind also operate on a larger scale in
the narrator's memoir. Having been so recently excluded from
the elite, but not wanting to think of himself as one of the
masses, he focuses particularly on the lower-middle-class
character of the noisy, unappealing crowds on the beach
('bürgerliches Kroppzeug' as he dismissively calls them, p.223),
thereby implying that the 'unpleasantness' of his memories of
them is somehow linked with the unpleasantness of Cipolla's
show. As has been noted, however, such people do not form the
bulk of Cipolla's audience, since they have mostly returned to
their native cities by the time he arrives in town. Similarly, the
magician's success in subjecting people from *various* nations to
his hypnotic influence does not bear out the suggestion
contained in the narrator's early stress on the Italian nature of
the crowds on the beach, namely that national characteristics
account for what happened on the holiday. In both cases the
selective focus of the narrator's memory has to do with his
suppressed and only gradually emerging guilt about his own
behaviour. By stressing the national and class characteristics of
the aggressive people he encounters on the beach, the narrator
casts himself in the role of an outside observer who has the
misfortune to be at the receiving end of such aggression. His
emphasis on what distinguishes him from the others on the
beach is a ruse — probably unconscious — to distract attention
from what he has in common with them, namely a disposition to
sado-masochistic behaviour, reflected in his case in his readiness
to defend the social elite that has humiliated him and which he
therefore resents.

Even the artistic and intellectual gifts of the narrator make
him the object of irony. As part of his general strategy of
emphasizing the things that distinguish him from the mass of the
others, the narrator recalls how bored he was by weeks of
unbroken sunshine, claiming that this somehow left 'tiefere,
uneinfachere Bedürfnisse der nordischen Seele' (p.222)
unsatisfied. Yet not only does this arrogance establish an
unintended parallel between his own complicated soul and

that of the magician clad in 'eine Art komplizierter Abendstraßeneleganz', it also makes a virtue of the very complexity which makes him so responsive to the ambivalent, mysterious figure of Cipolla, and, as a result, just as incapable of acting with moral decisiveness as the rest of Cipolla's victims.

Yet Mann's convoluted ironies do not even end with the ironical presentation of an ironical narrator, for this might leave the reader with a smug feeling of superiority over all the figures in the story. The narrator does have certain unacknowledged weaknesses which lead him to be spellbound by Cipolla, but without those weaknesses, without the bad conscience they stimulate, and the insights they give him into the weaknesses of others, he could not perform the invaluable task of bearing witness, as fully as he is able, to the actual experience of succumbing to the hypnotic, destructive fascination of a Cipolla. Would it have been better for him to have taken his family away from Torre di Venere as soon as the atmosphere of chauvinism made itself felt, or to have taken the protesting children away from Cipolla's show once he had realized how evil the man was? Perhaps so. But it is easy to be wise after the event, and it was not easy to predict where the minor annoyances of the holiday would lead. Had the narrator left the resort or the show earlier, there would have been no story, no report on the techniques of mass-manipulation, and no example of how difficult it is, even with good will and intelligence, to do the right thing. Without these things the story would lack perhaps the most important irony of all: that the reader, even with the benefits of hindsight and ironic distance, is given no guarantee that he will fare any better than the narrator when put to the test.

Bibliography

A. THOMAS MANN'S WRITINGS

1. *Achtung, Europa!* (Stockholm, Bermann-Fischer, 1938).
2. *Adel des Geistes* (Stockholm, Bermann-Fischer, 1948).
3. *Altes und Neues* (Frankfurt a.M., Fischer, 1953).
4. *Betrachtungen eines Unpolitischen* (Berlin, Fischer, 1919).
5. *Briefe, 1889-1936*, ed. Erika Mann (Frankfurt a.M., Fischer, 1961).
6. *Die Briefe Thomas Manns. Regesten und Register, Bd 1: Die Briefe von 1889 bis 1936*, ed. H. Bürgin and H.-O. Mayer (Frankfurt a.M., Fischer, 1976).
7. *Dichter über ihre Dichtungen. Thomas Mann, Teil II: 1918-1943*, ed. H. Wysling and M. Fischer (München, Heimeran/Fischer, 1979).
8. *Die Forderung des Tages* (Berlin, Fischer, 1930).
9. *Doktor Faustus* (Stockholm, Bermann-Fischer, 1947).
10. *Essays*, 3 vols, ed. Michael Mann (Frankfurt a.M., Fischer, 1977).
11. *Frage und Antwort. Interviews mit Thomas Mann*, ed. V. Hansen and G. Heine (Hamburg, Albrecht Knaus, 1983).
12. *Meine Zeit* (Amsterdam, Fischer, 1950).
13. *Pariser Rechenschaft* (Berlin, Fischer, 1926).
14. *Rede und Antwort* (Berlin, Fischer, 1922).
15. *Tagebücher 1933-1934*, ed. P. de Mendelssohn (Frankfurt a.M., Fischer, 1977).
16. 'Tragisches Reiseerlebnis', in *Velhagen und Klasings Monatshefte*, 44. Jg/April 1930/8. Heft. This is the first published version of the story which was later published in book form with the title *Mario und der Zauberer. Ein tragisches Reiseerlebnis*.
17. *Unordnung und frühes Leid und andere Erzählungen* (Frankfurt a.M., Fischer, 1987).
18. *Von deutscher Republik*, ed. H. Heibling (Frankfurt a.M., Fischer, 1984).

B. CRITICAL AND BACKGROUND LITERATURE

(i) Historical and political background

19. Bordeaux, Vahdah, *Benito Mussolini — the Man* (London, Hutchinson, 1927).
20. Deuerlein, Ernst (ed.), *Der Aufstieg der NSDAP in Augenzeugenberichten* (München, dtv, 1974).

21. Fabry, P.W., *Mutmaßungen über Hitler* (Düsseldorf, Bagel, 1969).
22. Fermi, Laura, *Mussolini* (London, University of Chicago Press, 1961).
23. Heiber, Helmut, *Joseph Goebbels* (München, dtv, 1965).
24. Hibbert, Christopher, *Benito Mussolini. A Biography* (London, Longman, 1962).
25. Hitler, Adolf, *Mein Kampf* (München, Verlag Franz Eher Nachfolger, 1933); also in translation by R. Manheim (London, Hutchinson, 1969).
26. King, Bolton, *Fascism in Italy* (London, Williams and Norgate, 1931).
27. Kirkpatrick, Ivone, *Mussolini. A Study in Power* (Connecticut, Greenwood, 1976).
28. Laqueur, Walter (ed.), *Fascism. A Reader's Guide* (Harmondsworth, Penguin, 1982).
29. Mack Smith, Denis, *Mussolini* (London, Weidenfeld and Nicolson, 1981).
30. Massock, Richard, *Italy from within* (London, Macmillan, 1943).
31. Nolte, Ernst (ed.), *Theorien über den Faschismus (Köln/Berlin, Kiepenheuer und Witsch, 1967)*.
32. Stern, J.P., *Hitler. The Führer and the People* (Glasgow, Fontana, 1975).
33. Weber, Eugen, *Varieties of Fascism* (New York, D. van Nostrand, 1964).

(ii) *Literary, philosophical and ideological background*
34. Bäumler, Alfred, *Das mythische Zeitalter* (München, Beck, 1965). Reprint of 1926 introduction to Bachofen's *Der Mythus von Orient und Occident*.
35. Benjamin, Walter, *Illuminationen* (Frankfurt a.M., Suhrkamp, 1961).
36. Freud, Sigmund, *Gesammelte Werke*, Vols 9 and 13 (London, Imago, 1940).
37. Goethe, Johann Wolfgang von, *Faust*, ed. E. Trunz (Hamburg, Wegner, 1963).
38. Klages, Ludwig, *Der Geist als Widersacher der Seele*, 3 vols (Leipzig, Barth, 1929-32).
39. Nietzsche, Friedrich, *Werke in drei Bänden*, ed. Karl Schlechta (München, Hanser, 1954).
40. Rosenberg, Alfred, *Der Mythus des zwanzigsten Jahrhunderts* (München, Hoheneichen, 1930).
41. Schopenhauer, Arthur, *Sämtliche Werke*, 7 vols (Leipzig, Brockhaus, 1937-41).
42. Spengler, Oswald, *Der Untergang des Abendlandes* (München, Beck, 1927).

(iii) *General literary criticism*
43. Baumgart, Reinhard, *Das Ironische und die Ironie in den Werken Thomas Manns* (München, Hanser, 1964).
44. Dierks, Manfred, *Studien zu Mythos und Psychologie bei Thomas Mann*, Thomas-Mann-Studien, 2 (Bern/München, Francke, 1972).

45. Hansen, Volkmar, *Thomas Mann* (Stuttgart, Metzler, 1984).
46. Jonas, Ilsedore, *Thomas Mann and Italy* (Tuscaloosa, University of Alabama Press, 1979).
47. Kurzke, Hermann, *Thomas-Mann-Forschung 1969-76*. Ein kritischer Bericht (Frankfurt a.M., Fischer, 1977).
48. Paulin, Roger, *The Brief Compass. The Nineteenth Century German Novelle* (Oxford, Clarendon Press, 1985).
49. Reed, T.J., *Thomas Mann. The Uses of Tradition* (Oxford, Oxford University Press, 1974).
50. Sautermeister, Gert, 'Thomas Mann: Der Ironiker als Citoyen. Politische Rhetorik und kritische Diagnose in der Weimarer Republik', in *Weimars Ende*, ed. T. Koebner (Frankfurt a.M., Suhrkamp, 1982), pp.271-302.
51. Seiler, Bernd, 'Ironischer Stil und realistischer Eindruck. Zu einem scheinbaren Widerspruch in der Erzählkunst Thomas Manns', *Deutsche Vierteljahresschrift für Literaturwissenschaft und Geistesgeschichte*, 60 (1986), 459-83.
52. Swales, Martin, *The German* Novelle (Princeton, Princeton University Press, 1977).
53. ——. *Thomas Mann. A Study (London, Heinemann, 1980).*
54. Wiese, Benno von, *Novelle*, 4th ed. (Stuttgart, Metzler, 1969).
55. Wysling, Hans, *Narzißmus und illusionäre Existenzform* (Bern/München, Francke, 1982).

(iv) *Commentaries on* Mario und der Zauberer
56. Bance, Alan, *Mann the Magician* or *The Good versus the Interesting*, Inaugural Lecture, University of Southampton, 1987.
57. ——. 'The Narrator in Thomas Mann's *Mario und der Zauberer*', *The Modern Language Review*, 82 (1987), 382-98.
58. Böhme, Hartmut, '*Mario und der Zauberer*. Positionen des Erzählers und Psychologie der Herrschaft', *Orbis Litterarum*, 30 (1975), 286-316.
59. Brinkmann, Karl, *Erläuterungen zu 'Mario und der Zauberer'* (Hollfeld, Bange, 1981).
60. Dierks, Manfred, 'Die Aktualität der positivistischen Methode am Beispiel Thomas Mann', *Orbis Litterarum*, 33 (1978), 158-82.
61. Diersen, Inge, *Untersuchungen zu Thomas Mann* (Berlin, Aufbau, 1959), pp.168-71.
62. Duffy, Charles and Don Keister, *'Mario and the Magician*. Two Letters by Thomas Mann', *Monatshefte (Wisconsin)*, 51 (1959), 190-92.
63. Eigler, F., 'Die ästhetische Inszenierung von Macht. Thomas Manns Novelle *Mario und der Zauberer*, *Heinrich Mann Jahrbuch*, 2 (1984), pp.172-83.
64. Freese, Wolfgang, 'Zum Verhältnis von Antifaschismus und Leseerwartung in *Mario und der Zauberer*', *Deutsche Vierteljahresschrift für Literaturwissenschaft und Geistesgeschichte*, 51 (1977), 659-75.

65. Garrin, Stephen, 'Thomas Mann's *Mario und der Zauberer*. Artistic Means and Didactic Ends', *Journal of English and Germanic Philology*, 77 (1978), 92-102.

66. Gray, Ronald, *The German Tradition in Literature, 1871-1945*, (Cambridge, Cambridge University Press, 1965), pp.173-84.

67. Grenville, Anthony, 'Idealism versus Materialism in the Representation of History in Literature. The Dictator Figure in Thomas Mann's *Mario und der Zauberer* and Brecht's *Der aufhaltsame Aufstieg des Arturo Ui*', *Journal of European Studies* (1987), 77-105.

68. Hartwig, Alfred, 'Problemhafte Gedanken zu Thomas Mann in Klasse 10', *Deutschunterricht* (Berlin), 28/3 (1975), 165-76.

69. Hatfield, Henry, 'Thomas Mann's *Mario und der Zauberer*. An Interpretation', *The Germanic Review*, 21 (1946), 306-12.

70. Hergershansen, Lore, 'Au sujet de *Mario und der Zauberer*. Cesare Gabrieli — Prototype de Cipolla?', *Etudes Germaniques*, 23 (1968), 268-75.

71. Imhof, Eugen, 'Thomas Mann: *Mario und der Zauberer*', *Der Deutschunterricht* (Stuttgart), 4 (1952), Heft 6, 59-69.

72. Koppen, Erwin, 'Schönheit, Tod und Teufel — Italienische Schauplätze im erzählenden Werk Thomas Manns', *arcadia*, 16 (1981), 151-67.

73. Leneau, Grant, '*Mario und der Zauberer*. The Narration of Seduction or the Seduction of Narration?', *Orbis Litterarum*, 40 (1985), 327-47.

74. Lukács, Georg, *Thomas Mann* (Berlin, Aufbau, 1953), *passim*.

75. Lunn, Eugene, 'Tales of Liberal Disquiet. Thomas Mann's *Mario and the Magician* and Interpretations of Fascism', *Literature and History*, 11/1 (1985), 77-100.

76. McIntyre, Alan, 'Determinism in *Mario und der Zauberer*', *The Germanic Review*, 52 (1977), 205-16.

77. ——. 'From Travemünde to Torre di Venere. Mannian Leitmotifs in Political Transition', *The Germanic Review*, 59 (1984), 26-31.

78. Maeda, Ryohei, 'Thomas Manns *Mario und der Zauberer*. Die Frage der Massen im Faschismus', *Doitsu Bungakuronko*, 10 (1968), 76-80.

79. Mandel, Siegfried, '*Mario and the Magician* or Who is Silvestra?', in *modern fiction studies* 25 (1979/80), 593-611.

80. Martin, J.S., 'Circean Seduction in Three Works by Thomas Mann', *Modern Language Notes*, 78 (1963), 346-52.

81. Matter, Harry, '*Mario und der Zauberer*. Die Bedeutung der Novelle im Schaffen Thomas Manns', *Weimarer Beiträge*, 6 (1960), 579-96.

82. Matenko, Percy, 'The Prototype of Cipolla in *Mario und der Zauberer*, *Italica*, 31 (1954), 133-35.

83. Mayer, Hans, *Thomas Mann. Werk und Entwicklung* (Berlin, Aufbau, 1950), pp.183-93.

84. Meyers, Jeffrey, 'Caligari and Cipolla. Mann's *Mario and the Magician*', *modern fiction studies* 32/2 (1986), 235-41.

85. Mieth, Annemarie, 'Unterrichtsmodell: Gattungs/Genrespezifik', *Deutschunterricht* (Berlin, 1972), 126-32.

86. Müller-Salget, Klaus, 'Der Tod in Torre di Venere. Spiegelung und
     Deutung des italienischen Faschismus in Thomas Manns *Mario und der
     Zauberer*', *arcadia*, 18 (1983), 50-65.
87. Pörnbacher, Karl (ed.), *Thomas Mann, 'Mario und der Zauberer'*.
     Erläuterungen und Dokumente (Stuttgart, Reclam, 1980).
88. Richter, Bernd, 'Psychologische Betrachtungen zu Thomas Manns
     Novelle *Mario und der Zauberer*', in *Vollendung und Größe Thomas
     Manns*, ed. G. Wenzel (Halle, Verlag Sprache und Literatur, 1962),
     pp.106-17.
89. Sautermeister, Gert, *Thomas Mann: 'Mario und der Zauberer'*
     (München, Fink, 1981).
90. Schwarz, Egon, 'Fascism and Society. Remarks on Thomas Mann's
     Novella *Mario and the Magician*', *Michigan Germanic Studies*,
     (1976), 47-67.
91. Speirs, R.C., 'Some psychological observations on domination,
     acquiescence and revolt in Thomas Mann's *Mario und der Zauberer*',
     Forum for Modern Language Studies, 16 (1980), 319-30.
92. Spelsberg, Helmut, *Thomas Manns Durchbruch zum Politischen in
     seinem kleinepischen Werk* (Marburg, Elwert, 1972), pp.31-83.
93. Vaget, Hans Rudolf, *Thomas Mann-Kommentar zu sämtlichen Erzähl-
     ungen* (München, Winkler, 1984), pp.220-249.
94. Wagener, Hans, 'Mann's Cipolla and Earlier Prototypes of the
     Magician' *Modern Language Notes*, 84 (1969), 800-02.
95. Wehner, James, 'The Nature of Evil in Melville's *Billy Budd* and
     Mann's *Mario und der Zauberer*', *The Comparatist* (1980), 31-34.
96. Weiß, Walter, 'Thomas Manns Kunst der sprachlichen und thematischen
     Integration', *Beihefte zur Zeitschrift 'Wirkendes Wort'*, 13 (1964).
97. Wuckel, Dieter, '*Mario und der Zauberer* in der zeitgenössischen
     Presseresonanz', in *Werk und Wirkung Thomas Manns in unserer
     Epoche*, ed. Helmut Brandt and Hans Kaufmann (Berlin/Weimar,
     Aufbau, 1978), pp.346-56.
98. Zimmermann, Werner, 'Thomas Mann: *Mario und der Zauberer*', in his
     Deutsche Prosadichtungen unseres Jahrhunderts, Teil I (Düsseldorf,
     Schwann, 1966), pp.274-95.